COMMON CORE

ENGLISH LANGUAGE ARTS

Activities that Captivate, Motivate, & Reinforce

Grade 8

by Jodie Fransen

IncentivePublications

BY WORLD BOOK

a Scott Fetzer company

Illustrated by Kathleen Bullock
Cover by Penny Laporte

Print Edition ISBN 978-1-62950-204-5
E-book Edition ISBN 978-1-62950-205-2 (PDF)

World Book, Inc.
233 North Michigan Avenue
Suite 2000
Chicago, Illinois, 60601 U.S.A.

For information about World Book and Incentive Publications products, call **1-800-967-5325,** or visit our websites at **www.worldbook.com** and **www.incentivepublications.com.**

Printed in the United States by Sheridan Books, Inc.
Chelsea, Michigan
1st Printing March 2014

CONTENTS

3

Great Support for Common Core State Standards!

Invite your students to join in on adventures and mysteries with colorful characters. The high-appeal topics and illustrations will spark their interest as they

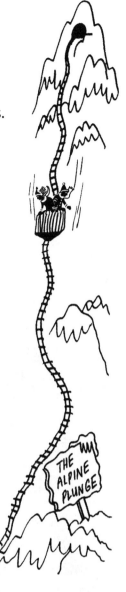

... thrill to the dangers (and risks) of such amusement park attractions as the Terminator, the Stomach Wrencher, and the Heartstopper,

... help a baffled detective solve "The Case of the Serial Bather,"

... witness a colossal school cafeteria food fight,

... try to outwit Captain Blackbeard on a race to find pirate treasure,

... hang out with tarantulas and King Arthur's knights,

... watch the development of "The Great Linguine Disaster,"

... discover the truth about the world's longest banana split,

... ponder the ups and downs of romance with heartbroken characters,

... weigh in on arguments about sagging pants and dress codes,

... hear some convincing tales of UFO sightings,

... and tackle many other engaging ventures.

And while they follow these escapades, they will be moving toward competence in critical language skills that they need for success in the real world.

How to Use This Book

- The pages are tools to support your teaching of the concepts, processes, and skills outlined in the Common Core State Standards. This is not a curriculum; it is a collection of intriguing experiences to use as you work with your students or children.

- Use any given page to introduce, explain, teach, practice, extend, assess, provide independent work for, start a discussion about, or get students collaborating on a standard, skill, or concept.

- Use any page in a large-group or small-group setting to deepen understandings and expand knowledge and skills.

- Pages are **not** intended for use solely as independent work. Do the activities together or review and discuss the work together.

- Each activity is focused on a particular standard or cluster of standards. However, most pages use or can be expanded to strengthen other standards as well.

- The book is organized according to the Common Core language strands. Use the tables on pages 9 to 19, the page labels, and notations on the Contents pages to identify the standards supported by each page.

- For further mastery of Common Core State Standards, see the suggestions on page 8.

About Common Core English Language Arts Standards

The Common Core State Standards for English Language Arts at the middle-grades level aim to build strong content knowledge across a wide range of subject areas. They are also designed to develop capabilities for thoughtful use of technology and digital media; for finding, applying, and evaluating evidence; for working and thinking independently; and for deepening reasoning and understanding. To best help students gain and master these robust standards for reading, writing, speaking, listening, and language:

1. Know the standards well. Keep them in front of you. Understand for yourself the big picture of what the standards seek to do. (See www.corestandards.org.)

2. Work to apply, expand, and deepen student skills. With activities in this book (or with any other learning activities), plan to include

   . . . collaboration with peers in pairs, small groups, and large groups.

   . . . plenty of discussion and integration of language content.

   . . . emphasis on asking questions, analyzing, careful reading and listening, finding evidence, and reasoning.

   . . . lots of observation, meaningful feedback, follow-up, and reflection.

3. Ask questions that advance reasoning, discernment, relevance, and real-life connection:

- *Why? What does this mean?*
- *How do you know?*
- *What led you to this conclusion?*
- *Where did you find this?*
- *What else do you know (or need to know)?*
- *What is the evidence?*
- *Where else could you look?*
- *How is _____ like (or unlike) _____?*
- *What would another viewpoint be?*
- *What does the text infer?*
- *What is the purpose of the presentation?*
- *What beliefs lie behind the writer's claims? How can you tell?*
- *Do you agree? Why or why not?*
- *How does this part affect that part?*
- *Where have you seen something like this before?*
- *How does the structure of the text affect the message?*

- *What are the parts? How do they work together?*
- *How does the text confirm your ideas?*
- *How would this vary for a different purpose, place, person, or situation?*
- *How does the idea of the text (or speech or argument) build?*
- *How is this idea affected by the ideas that came before it?*
- *How could you write (or say) this to give _____ effect?*
- *What is the effect of using this word (or phrase, or idea, or structure)?*
- *What is the writer's (or speaker's) viewpoint or bias? How can you tell?*
- *So what? (What difference does this information, or perspective, or discovery make?)*

College and Career Readiness Anchor Standards (CCRS)
for Reading, Grades K-12

Anchor Standard	Standard	Pages that Support
Key Ideas and Details		
CCRA.R.1	Read closely to determine what the text says explicitly and to make logical inferences from it; cite specific textual evidence when writing or speaking to support conclusions drawn from the text.	22-23, 24, 25, 26-27, 28, 29, 30-31, 32, 33, 34, 35, 36-37, 38-39, 40, 41, 42, 44, 45, 46, 47, 48-49, 50, 51, 52-53, 54, 55, 56-57, 58-59, 60-61, 62-63, 64
CCRA.R.2	Determine central ideas or themes of a text and analyze their development; summarize the key supporting details and ideas.	25, 26-27, 28, 47, 48-49, 50, 60-61, 62-63, 64
CCRA.R.3	Analyze how and why individuals, events, and ideas develop and interact over the course of a text.	29, 30-31, 51, 52-53
Craft and Structure		
CCRA.R.4	Interpret words and phrases as they are used in a text, including determining technical, connotative, and figurative meanings, and analyze how specific word choices shape meaning or tone.	32, 33, 34, 35, 52-53, 54, 55, 56-57, 58-59
CCRA.R.5	Analyze the structure of texts, including how specific sentences, paragraphs, and larger portions of the text (e.g., a section, chapter, scene, or stanza) relate to each other and the whole.	36-37, 56-57
CCRA.R.6	Assess how point of view or purpose shapes the content and style of a text.	38, 41, 58-59
Integration of Knowledge and Ideas		
CCRA.R.7	Integrate and evaluate content presented in diverse media and formats, including visually and quantitatively, as well as in words.	42, 64
CCRA.R.8	Delineate and evaluate the argument and specific claims in a text, including the validity of the reasoning as well as the relevance and sufficiency of the evidence.	60-61, 62-63
CCRA.R.9	Analyze how two or more texts address similar themes or topics in order to build knowledge or to compare the approaches the authors take.	38-39, 40, 41, 62-63
Range of Reading and Level of Text Complexity		
CCRA.R.10	Read and comprehend complex literary and informational texts independently and proficiently.	22-42, 44-64

College and Career Readiness Anchor Standards (CCRS)
for Writing, Grades K-12

Anchor Standard	Standard	Pages that Support
Text Types and Purposes		
CCRA.W.1	Write arguments to support claims in an analysis of substantive topics or texts, using valid reasoning and relevant and sufficient evidence.	66-68
CCRA.W.2	Write informative/explanatory texts to examine and convey complex ideas and information clearly and accurately through the effective selection, organization, and analysis of content.	69-71
CCRA.W.3	Write narratives to develop real or imagined experiences or events using effective technique, well-chosen details, and well-structured event sequences.	72-74
Production and Distribution of Writing		
CCRA.W.4	Produce clear and coherent writing in which the development, organization, and style are appropriate to task, purpose, and audience.	66-68, 69-71, 72-74, 75, 76, 77, 79-81, 82-83, 84
CCRA.W.5	Develop and strengthen writing as needed by planning, revising, editing, rewriting, or trying a new approach.	75, 78, 79-81
CCRA.W.6	Use technology, including the Internet, to produce and publish writing and to interact and collaborate with others.	79-81 *See note below.*
Research to Build and Present Knowledge		
CCRA.W.7	Conduct short as well as more sustained research projects based on focused questions, demonstrating understanding of the subject under investigation.	79-81
CCRA.W.8	Gather relevant information from multiple print and digital sources, assess the credibility and accuracy of each source, and integrate the information while avoiding plagiarism.	79-81
CCRA.W.9	Draw evidence from literary or informational texts to support analysis, reflection, and research.	82-84
Range of Writing		
CCRA.W.10	Write routinely over extended time frames (time for research, reflection, and revision) and shorter time frames (a single sitting or a day or two) for a range of tasks, purposes, and audiences.	66-84

Standard 6: *Use technology as a part of your approach for any of the activities in this writing section. Students can create, dictate, photograph, scan, enhance with art or color, or share any of the products they create as a part of these pages.*

Writing Standards, Grade 8

ELA Standard	Standard	Pages that Support
Text Types and Purposes		
W.8.1	Write arguments to support claims with clear reasons and relevant evidence.	66-68
W.8.1a	Introduce claim(s), acknowledge and distinguish the claim(s) from alternate or opposing claims, and organize the reasons and evidence logically.	66-68
W.8.1b	Support claim(s) with logical reasoning and relevant evidence, using accurate, credible sources and demonstrating an understanding of the topic or text.	66-68
W.8.1c	Use words, phrases, and clauses to create cohesion and clarify the relationships among claim(s), counterclaims, reasons, and evidence.	66-68
W.8.1d	Establish and maintain a formal style.	66-68
W.8.1e	Provide a concluding statement or section that follows from and supports the argument presented.	66-68
W.8.2	Write informative/explanatory texts to examine a topic and convey ideas, concepts, and information through the selection, organization, and analysis of relevant content.	69-71
W.8.2a	Introduce a topic clearly, previewing what is to follow; organize ideas, concepts, and information into broader categories; include formatting (e.g., headings), graphics (e.g., charts, tables), and multimedia when useful to aiding comprehension.	69-71
W.8.2b	Develop the topic with relevant, well-chosen facts, definitions, concrete details, quotations, or other information and examples.	69-71
W.8.2c	Use appropriate transitions to create cohesion and clarify the relationships among ideas and concepts.	69-71
W.8.2d	Use precise language and domain-specific vocabulary to inform about or explain the topic.	69-71
W.8.2e	Establish and maintain a formal style.	69-71
W.8.2f	Provide a concluding statement or section that follows from and supports the information or explanation presented.	69-71
W.8.3	Write narratives to develop real or imagined experiences or events using effective technique, descriptive details, and clear event sequences.	72-74
W.8.3a	Engage and orient the reader by establishing a context and point of view and introducing a narrator and/or characters; organize an event sequence that unfolds naturally and logically.	72-74
W.8.3b	Use narrative techniques, such as dialogue, pacing, description, and reflection to develop experiences, events, and/or characters.	72-74
W.8.3c	Use a variety of transition words, phrases, and clauses to convey sequence and signal shifts from one time frame or setting to another.	72-74
W.8.3d	Use precise words and phrases, relevant descriptive details, and sensory language to capture the action and convey experiences and events.	72-74
W.8.3e	Provide a conclusion that follows from and reflects on the narrated experiences or events.	72-74

Common Core Reinforcement Activities — 8th Grade Language

Writing standards continue on next page.

Writing Standards, Grade 8, continued

ELA Standard	Standard	Pages that Support
Production and Distribution of Writing		
W.8.4	Produce clear and coherent writing in which the development, organization, and style are appropriate to task, purpose, and audience. (Grade-specific expectations for writing types are defined in standards 1–3 above.)	66-68, 69-71, 72-74, 75, 76, 77, 79-81, 82-83, 84
W.8.5	With some guidance and support from peers and adults, develop and strengthen writing as needed by planning, revising, editing, rewriting, or trying a new approach, focusing on how well purpose and audience have been addressed. (Editing for conventions should demonstrate command of Language standards 1–3 up to and including grade 8 here.)	75, 78, 79-81
W.8.6	Use technology, including the Internet, to produce and publish writing and present the relationships between information and ideas efficiently as well as to interact and collaborate with others.	79-81 *See note below.*
Research to Build and Present Knowledge		
W.8.7	Conduct short research projects to answer a question (including a self-generated question), drawing on several sources and generating additional related, focused questions that allow for multiple avenues of exploration.	79-81
W.8.8	Gather relevant information from multiple print and digital sources, using search terms effectively; assess the credibility and accuracy of each source; and quote or paraphrase the data and conclusions of others while avoiding plagiarism and following a standard format for citation.	79-81
W.8.9	Draw evidence from literary or informational texts to support analysis, reflection, and research.	82-84
W.8.9a	Apply grade 8 reading standards to literature (e.g., "Analyze how a modern work of fiction draws on themes, patterns of events, or character types from myths, traditional stories, or religious works such as the Bible, including describing how the material is rendered new").	82-83
W.8.9b	Apply grade 8 reading standards to literary nonfiction (e.g., "Delineate and evaluate the argument and specific claims in a text, assessing whether the reasoning is sound and the evidence is relevant and sufficient; recognize when irrelevant evidence is introduced").	84
Range of Writing		
W.8.10	Write routinely over extended time frames (time for research, reflection, and revision) and shorter time frames (a single sitting or a day or two) for a range of discipline-specific tasks, purposes, and audiences.	66-84

Standard 6: *Use technology as a part of your approach for any of the activities in this writing section. Students can create, dictate, photograph, scan, enhance with art or color, or share any of the products they create as a part of these pages.*

College and Career Readiness Anchor Standards (CCRS) for Speaking and Listening, Grades K-12

Anchor Standard	Standard	Pages that Support
Comprehension and Collaboration		
CCRA.SL.1	Prepare for and participate effectively in a range of conversations and collaborations with diverse partners, building on others' ideas and expressing their own clearly and persuasively.	86, 87, 88, 89
CCRA.SL.2	Integrate and evaluate information presented in diverse media and formats, including visually, quantitatively, and orally.	90, 91, 92, 93, 94
CCRA.SL.3	Evaluate a speaker's point of view, reasoning, and use of evidence and rhetoric.	90, 91, 92, 93, 94, 97, 98
Presentation of Knowledge and Ideas		
CCRA.SL.4	Present information, findings, and supporting evidence such that listeners can follow the line of reasoning and the organization, development, and style are appropriate to task, purpose, and audience.	95, 96, 97, 98
CCRA.SL.5	Make strategic use of digital media and visual displays of data to express information and enhance understanding of presentations.	95, 96
CCRA.SL.6	Adapt speech to a variety of contexts and communicative tasks, demonstrating command of formal English when indicated or appropriate.	86-98

Note on range and content of student speaking and listening:

To build a foundation for college and career readiness, students must have ample opportunities to take part in a variety of rich, structured conversations—as part of a whole class, in small groups, and with a partner. Being productive members of these conversations requires that students contribute accurate, relevant information; respond to and develop what others have said; make comparisons and contrasts; and analyze and synthesize a multitude of ideas in various domains.

New technologies have broadened and expanded the role that speaking and listening play in acquiring and sharing knowledge and have tightened their link to other forms of communication. Digital texts confront students with the potential for continually updated content and dynamically changing combinations of words, graphics, images, hyperlinks, and embedded video and audio.

Speaking and Listening Standards: The speaking and listening standards are not specifically addressed in this book. However, most pages can be used for conversation and collaboration. Teachers and parents are encouraged to use the activities in a sharing and discussion format. Many of the pages include visual information that students can include in the integration and evaluation of information.

In addition, most of the texts and activities can be adapted to listening activities or can be used to support the listening and speaking standards.

Speaking and Listening Standards, Grade 8

ELA Standard	Standard	Pages that Support
Comprehension and Collaboration		
SL8.1	Engage effectively in a range of collaborative discussions (one-on-one, in groups, and teacher-led) with diverse partners on Grade 8 topics, texts, and issues, building on others' ideas and expressing their own clearly.	86-89
SL8.1a	Come to discussions prepared, having read or researched material under study; explicitly draw on that preparation by referring to evidence on the topic, text, or issue to probe and reflect on ideas under discussion.	86, 87, 88, 89
SL8.1b	Follow rules for collegial discussions and decision-making, track progress toward specific goals and deadlines, and define individual roles as needed.	86, 87, 88, 89
SL8.1c	Pose questions that connect the ideas of several speakers and respond to others' questions and comments with relevant evidence, observations, and ideas.	86, 87, 88, 89
SL8.1d	Acknowledge new information expressed by others and, when warranted, modify their own views.	86, 87, 88, 89
SL8.2	Analyze the purpose of information presented in diverse media and formats (e.g., visually, quantitatively, orally) and evaluate the motives (e.g., social, commercial, political) behind its presentation.	90, 91, 92, 93, 94
SL8.3	Delineate a speaker's argument and specific claims, evaluating the soundness of the reasoning and relevance and sufficiency of the evidence and identifying when irrelevant evidence is introduced.	90, 91, 93, 94
Presentation of Knowledge and Ideas		
SL8.4	Present claims and findings, emphasizing salient points in a focused, coherent manner with relevant evidence, sound valid reasoning, and well-chosen details; use appropriate eye contact, adequate volume, and clear pronunciation.	95, 96, 97, 98
SL8.5	Integrate multimedia and visual displays into presentations to clarify information, strengthen claims and evidence, and add interest.	95, 96
SL8.6	Adapt speech to a variety of contexts and tasks, demonstrating command of formal English when indicated or appropriate. (See grade 8 language standards 1 and 3 here for specific expectations.)	86-99

16

College and Career Readiness Anchor Standards (CCRS) for Language, Grades K-12

Anchor Standard	Standard	Pages that Support
Conventions of Standard English		
CCRA.L.1	Demonstrate command of the conventions of standard English grammar and usage when writing or speaking.	100-107
CCRA.L.2	Demonstrate command of the conventions of standard English capitalization, punctuation, and spelling when writing.	108-111
Knowledge of Language		
CCRA.L.3	Apply knowledge of language to understand how language functions in different contexts, to make effective choices for meaning or style, and to comprehend more fully when reading or listening.	100-111
Vocabulary Acquisition and Use		
CCRA.L.4	Determine or clarify the meaning of unknown and multiple-meaning words and phrases by using context clues, analyzing meaningful word parts, and consulting general and specialized reference materials, as appropriate.	112-126
CCRA.L.5	Demonstrate understanding of figurative language, word relationships, and nuances in word meanings.	122-125
CCRA.L.6	Acquire and use accurately a range of general academic and domain-specific words and phrases sufficient for reading, writing, speaking, and listening at the college and career readiness level; demonstrate independence in gathering vocabulary knowledge when encountering an unknown term important to comprehension or expression.	126

Note on range and content of student language use:

To build a foundation for college and career readiness in language, students must gain control over many conventions of standard English grammar, usage, and mechanics as well as learn other ways to use language to convey meaning effectively. They must also be able to determine or clarify the meaning of grade-appropriate words encountered through listening, reading, and media use; come to appreciate that words have nonliteral meanings, shadings of meaning, and relationships to other words; and expand their vocabulary in the course of studying content. The inclusion of language standards in their own strand should not be taken as an indication that skills related to conventions, effective language use, and vocabulary are unimportant to reading, writing, speaking, and listening; indeed, they are inseparable from such contexts.

Language Standards, Grade 8

ELA Standard	Standard	Pages that Support
Conventions of Standard English		
L.8.1	Demonstrate command of the conventions of standard English grammar and usage when writing or speaking.	100-107
L.8.1a	Explain the function of verbals (gerunds, participles, infinitives) in general and their function in particular sentences.	100, 101
L.8.1b	Form and use verbs in the active and passive voice.	102, 103
L.8.1c	Form and use verbs in the indicative, imperative, interrogative, conditional, and subjunctive mood.	104-105, 106, 107
L.8.1d	Recognize and correct inappropriate shifts in verb voice and mood.	107
L.8.2	Demonstrate command of the conventions of standard English capitalization, punctuation, and spelling when writing.	108-111
L.8.2a	Use punctuation (comma, ellipsis, dash) to indicate a pause or break.	108, 109
L.8.2b	Use an ellipsis to indicate an omission.	109
L.8.2c	Spell correctly.	110, 111
Knowledge of Language		
L.8.3	Use knowledge of language and its conventions when writing, speaking, reading, or listening.	112
L.8.3a	Use verbs in the active and passive voice and in the conditional and subjunctive mood to achieve particular effects (e.g., emphasizing the actor or the action; expressing uncertainty or describing a state contrary to fact).	112

Language standards continue on next page.

Language Standards, Grade 8, continued

ELA Standard	Standard	Pages that Support
Vocabulary Acquisition and Use		
L.8.4	Determine or clarify the meaning of unknown and multiple-meaning words and phrases based on grade 8 reading and content, choosing flexibly from a range of strategies.	112-115, 117, 119-124
L.8.4a	Use context (e.g., the overall meaning of a sentence or paragraph; a word's position or function in a sentence) as a clue to the meaning of a word or phrase.	112, 113, 114, 115, 117, 119, 120, 121, 123, 124
L.8.4b	Use common, grade-appropriate Greek or Latin affixes and roots as clues to the meaning of a word (e.g., precede, recede, secede).	115, 116
L.8.4c	Consult general and specialized reference materials (e.g., dictionaries, glossaries, thesauruses), both print and digital, to find the pronunciation of a word or determine or clarify its precise meaning or its part of speech.	117, 118
L.8.4d	Verify the preliminary determination of the meaning of a word or phrase (e.g., by checking the inferred meaning in context or in a dictionary).	119
L.8.5	Demonstrate understanding of figurative language, word relationships, and nuances in word meanings.	120-125
L.8.5a	Interpret figures of speech (e.g., verbal irony, puns) in context.	120, 121
L.8.5b	Use the relationship between particular words to better understand each of the words.	122, 123
L.8.5c	Distinguish among the connotations (associations) of words with similar denotations (definitions) (e.g., bullheaded, willful, firm, persistent, resolute).	124, 125
L.8.6	Acquire and use accurately grade-appropriate general academic and domain-specific words and phrases; gather vocabulary knowledge when considering a word or phrase important to comprehension or expression.	126

READING

LITERATURE

Grade 8

THE PASTA INCIDENT

What happened at Pasta Piatti was the talk of the town for months.

Read the story and the menu. Then answer the questions and follow the directions on the next page (page 23).

It was to be the paramount night of Joe's career as a top chef in this big city. Tonight, he would be serving all 50 state governors. His restaurant was chosen as the spot for their banquet solely because of Joe's reputation—especially the reputation for his famous linguine.

Everything was ready. The guests were already enjoying the pâté. Joe's minestrone had never been so full of flavor, the tiramisu was perfect, and each *insalata caprese* was ready to be placed in front of a governor. The marinara sauce was simmering in a mammoth pot, its sweet basil aroma steaming up the kitchen. As Joe was busy testing and stirring the sauce, he directed his son, Mario, to drop the linguine noodles into the large pot of boiling water. Mario had just fallen in love that day and was not paying attention in his usual focused manner. Instead of 19 packages of noodles, Mario put 91 packages into the boiling water. That was the beginning of the greatest linguine disaster in the history of the city.

Joe Giacomini's Pasta Piatti Menu

Governors' Dinner, March 10, 2013

Antipasto
Pâté Dolce Vita

Zuppe
Minestrone Giacomini

Pasta
Linguine with Marinara Sauce, Basil Pesto, and Sweet Sun-Dried Tomato Italian Sausage

Frutti de Mare
Shrimp & Lobster Scampi a la Napoletana

Insalata Caprese
Fresh Buffalo Mozzarella, Heirloom Tomatoes, and Basil

Dolce
Tiramisu

Name

THE PASTA INCIDENT, continued

Use the story and the menu on page 22 to answer the questions.

1. What clues reveal the importance of this dinner for Joe and his restaurant?

2. What clues reveal the kind of restaurant?

3. How does the author let you know that some sort of an incident is about to happen?

4. What is the meaning of the following words in the story or on the menu?

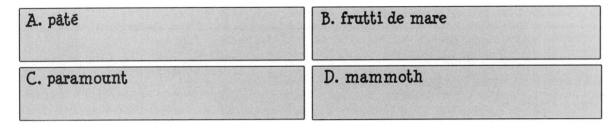

| A. pâté | B. frutti de mare |
| C. paramount | D. mammoth |

Now use what you read in the story to decide what happens next. Write your conclusion to the story on this page. Keep your story and writing style consistent with what has happened so far.

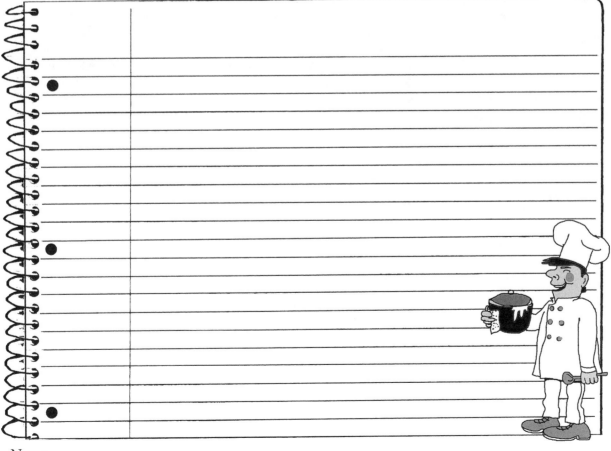

Name

A POISON TREE

Are you ever angry with a friend (or anyone else for that matter)? Read this poem, written by famous English poet William Blake over 200 years ago. Maybe it will give you some ideas about what to do with your anger.

Analyzing a piece of literature requires that you provide evidence from the text to support your ideas. Use evidence to support each of your answers below.

A Poison Tree
by William Blake

I was angry with my friend:
I told my wrath, my wrath did end.
I was angry with my foe:
I told it not, my wrath did grow.
And I watered it in fears,
Night and morning with my tears;
And I sunned it with smiles,
And with soft deceitful wiles.
And it grew both day and night,
Till it bore an apple bright.
And my foe beheld it shine.
And he knew that it was mine,
And into my garden stole
When the night had veiled the pole*;
In the morning glad I see
My foe outstretched beneath the tree.

pole means *sky*

Work cited:
Blake, William. "A Poison Tree." *Songs of Innocence and Experience, with Other Poems.* London: Basil Montagu Pickering, 1866. *Google Books*. Web. 7 Nov. 2013.

1. What is the poet's main message?

2. How does the poem title connect to the message?

3. Why did the foe come into the garden?

4. What was the result of the growth of the poison tree?

5. What is the meaning of these words or phrases?

A. wrath	B. deceitful wiles
C. foe	D. veiled

Name

A FAMILIAR THEME

"Your Cheatin' Heart" has a theme that is familiar in middle schools and is probably a topic you have encountered. The theme of a story is its central idea. It might be directly stated or it might be implied within a story.

As you read this story, look for the theme and for the way the author develops it through the characters, setting, and plot. Then answer the questions below.

Your Cheatin' Heart

When Jenny happened to walk past the table where Serena and Anne sat in the cafeteria, she heard sobbing. Jenny didn't mean to eavesdrop, but she couldn't help overhearing.

"What am I supposed to do?" Choking back tears, Anne lamented to her friend, "I can't fail this exam. I just don't understand the material! There's no way I'm going to learn this science before next period. My parents will be so disappointed—and I'll lose my driving privileges!"

Jenny knew that Serena and Anne were inseparable friends. Both were honor students and leaders in student government. What a bad break for Anne if she couldn't grasp some of the concepts in their science class!

Serena, good friend that she was, hugged Anne, assuring her, "It will be okay. "We'll find a way. You'll pass the test. I won't let you fail."

Jenny wondered how the girls could pull off such a task. Surely they wouldn't cheat! Serena's dad was an administrator at their school. If she got caught cheating, she'd be in big trouble!

Jenny's worst fears were realized when the teacher passed out the science tests. Serena cleverly positioned herself to make sure that Anne could see her paper. It seemed certain that their plan was to let Anne copy Serena's answers. Jenny decided to keep a silent watch during the exam.

1. What is the theme of the story?

2. Circle phrases or sentences in the story that provide evidence of the theme.

3. What is Jenny's role in the conflict of the story?

4. What is the effect of the way the author chose to end the story by not telling the reader the final outcome?

Name

A BIZARRE CASE, INDEED

When you analyze a story, you decide how each part of it contributes to its message and its effect on the reader. Enjoy your examination of this odd mystery!

As you read the story, pay attention to the theme (central message) and the way it develops through the setting, plot, and character development. Then follow the directions on the next page (page 27).

The Case of the Serial Bather

It was after the third incident that Detective Razor was asked to take on the cases. Right away, he could see that something strange was happening in Oak Grove. Citizens had called the police with reports that they had come home to find dirty bathtubs with greasy rings left around them. While he was amused, Detective Razor was also concerned enough to investigate the cases thoroughly.

The detective took statements from all affected homeowners. In each case, after being away on vacation, they had returned to find a tub full of dirty water, a bathtub ring, a wet and dirty bath mat, and many long blonde hairs around the tub and bathroom.

Over the next three weeks, the police station continued to receive calls. The reports were always the same. The scene was always the same. The evidence was always the same.

For a while, the detective was stumped. What a strange crime! Why would someone want to take a bath in other people's homes? Was it someone who had no bathtub? How did the bather know that the people were away? Why was there no sign of breaking and entering at any of the houses? Razor could see only two links among the cases: the incidents occurred while the homeowners were away and each home had a pet that was left at home.

The detective decided to follow a hunch. With little trouble, he convinced his neighbor, Jane Green, to take a vacation. Jane made all her arrangements and left town. Razor carefully slipped into Jane's home and settled into the bathroom closet with his lunch and a pillow. He waited.

Early the next morning, he heard a key in the back door. Jane's puppy, Cocoa, barked excitedly. Razor heard more barking and scampering of feet. Soon the bathroom door opened. "Okay, Lucy, time for your bath," came a young man's voice. A teenage boy filled the tub with warm water, added some liquid soap, and helped an old, longhaired, blonde dog into the tub. "You soak while I feed and walk Cocoa. When I come back, you'll be nice and clean." The big dog was left to bathe while the dog-walker did his job with the vacationer's pet.

The case was solved!

Looks like a clue!

Name

A BIZARRE CASE, INDEED, CONTINUED

Use the story "The Case of the Serial Bather" to answer these questions.

Setting

What is the primary setting (or the primary settings)?

What effect does the setting have on the plot?

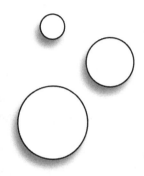

Main Character

Who is the main character in this story?

Write three adjectives to describe the main character.

What effect does this character have on the plot?

Theme

What is the theme?

How can you tell?

Plot

The plot of a story is the sequence of events (what happens).

Write a summary of the plot (in no more than three sentences).

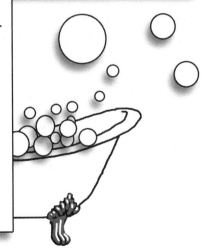

Use with page 26.

Name

Common Core Reinforcement Activities — 8th Grade Language

THE REASON FOR ADOLESCENCE

No doubt you have wondered about the reasons for many things. This poet pondered the reason for adolescence.

Look for the writer's main message and the way she conveys it.

The reason for adolescence is difficult to see
It's not for making parents happy and fulfilled.
It seems only to bring them grief.
It's not a time for beauty . . .
What with skin that lumps and bumps
And bodies that burst out in awkward ways.

It's not for deep friendships . . .
For some friends
...leave
...let you down
...betray you
...trade you in for someone more important.

It's not for building self-esteem . . .
There's always someone who is
...smarter
...prettier
...thinner
...cooler
...more popular
...or better at the sport that is your best.

It's not for gaining respect and admiration . . .
Teenagers don't get much of that.
It's not hard to miss the sour face of the restaurant owner when a group of adolescents drops in for a meal.
It's not hard to catch the stiffening posture and increased alertness of the salesperson when a teenager walks into a clothing shop.
The reason for adolescence, though difficult to see, is this: for an adolescent to be what only an adolescent can be . . .
. . . an invitation to children — someone they can look forward to being
. . . and a reminder to adults of who they were, what they did, and maybe who they wish they could be again.

by Stephanie, Grade 9

What is the theme of the poem?

Circle words or phrases in the poem as evidence of your choice.

Name

WHO?

Dialogue (a conversation between two people) can serve a variety of purposes in literature and drama. One of television's most famous dialogues came in the form of a comedy routine called "Who's on First?" by the very funny team of Bud Abbott and Lou Costello.

Use the Internet to find this famous routine. It will be easy to find an audio version of the actual event as well as a written transcript. After listening and reading, fill in the information on the baseball shapes.

1.
The main misunderstanding between the two characters

2.
Description of Abbott's character (the coach)

What?

A+C

4.
Cause of Costello's frustration

3.
Description of Costello's character (the interviewer)

Who?

A+C

5.
What would happen to this story if it were retold in narrative form (without dialogue)?

6.
Why do you think this routine became such a classic?

Name _____

Common Core Reinforcement Activities — 8th Grade Language

"HOW TERRIBLY TRAGIC," SOBBED THE READER

This title says it all! This is exactly how a writer wants his or her reader to respond to a sad story. One of the saddest stories of all time is the love story of Pyramus and Thisbe. It is retold below in narrative form without any dialogue.

As you read, think of the words the characters might actually be saying. Then follow the directions on the next page (page 31).

Long ago, there were two young lovers who lived next door to one another. Sadly, an exceedingly thick wall divided the two properties, and the lovers were forbidden by their parents to see one another. However, as is most often the case, true love finds a way, and the lovers talked in secret by communicating through a small chink in the great wall. One night, as the two lovers met in the shadows, they made a daring plan.

Pyramus told Thisbe that he could no longer live without the freedom to see her. Thisbe said that she was also longing to be with Pyramus—to see him and talk to him without fear of being discovered. Pyramus replied that he had thought of a way that they could meet. Thisbe was eager to hear his plan. Pyramus

explained that, on the next holy day, each would get permission from his or her parents to visit the chapel in a nearby park to say prayers. He said that, near the chapel, was a lovely tree with thick, white blossoms. He explained that Thisbe should meet him there, just as the chapel bells struck three o'clock. Thisbe agreed excitedly. She dreamed aloud about how they would then run off together and be married and live happily ever after.

Tragically, Thisbe went to the chapel early. As she arrived, a lion met her on the path. Frightened, she ran to hide behind the chapel to wait for Pyramus. In her flight, she lost her veil, which was picked up by the lion who had just finished a bloody dinner. As Pyramus approached at the three o'clock bell, he observed the lion tearing at the now-bloody veil. Of course, he assumed that the lion's dinner had been his precious Thisbe. Distraught with guilt that he had brought his lover to such a violent death, he took a knife from his belt and stabbed himself. As he lay dying, Thisbe peered out from her hiding place. She ran to Pyramus, but only in time to hear his last words of devotion for her. Finally united with her lover, she could not let him die alone. She took the knife from his hands and stabbed herself in the heart. The two lay together under the lovely tree whose white blossoms turned red as they drew the lovers' blood from the earth. The tree stands as a memorial to them, even to this day.

Name

Use with page 31.

30

"HOW TERRIBLY TRAGIC," SOBBED THE READER, CONTINUED

After reading the story on page 30, follow the directions below.

1. Write some words or phrases the author used to develop the character of Pyramus.

2. Write some words or phrases the author used to develop the character of Thisbe.

3. The middle section of the story (written in italics) describes conversations between Pyramus and Thisbe. Now make the story come alive by rewriting the paragraph in dialogue form. The dialogue must be true to the story, but try to make the conversation as interesting and suspenseful as possible. Be sure to use proper punctuation and paragraph breaks so that the story flows easily and the reader can clearly tell who is speaking. Otherwise, your reader won't be sobbing at the end!

Name

Use with page 30.

MALAPROPISMS ON THE LOOSE

Back in 1775, playwright Richard Sheridan wrote *The Rivals,* a comedy about manners. The main character, Mrs. Malaprop, often used a wrong word that sounded similar to the word that would have been correct. This type of word misuse came to be known as a malapropism. Unwittingly, people often substitute a word that has a different meaning—making for fun (and sometimes embarrassing) mistakes.

Catch the misused words in these sentences. Circle each one and write the correct word nearby.

2.
I congratulate each of you for having extinguished yourselves.

3.
This score is unparalyzed in the team's history.

4.
Winston Churchill was a man of great statue.

1.
Are you and Sam having fun riding that tantrum bicycle?

5.
Mom hired a tudor to give me extra help with math.

6. I can hardly breathe because my sciences are infected.

7. The fire alarm is ringing! We must evaporate the school.

8. We just finished a lesson about proper punctuation for contraptions.

9. Putrefied, the students screamed when the monster entered the classroom.

10. We all laughed historically at my mother's new hairdo.

11. In Oregon, the law requires that Presbyterians have the right of way over vehicles.

12. Governments ruled by kings and queens are called mockeries.

13. There was little water, so farmers had to irritate their crops.

14. Write your own sentence with a malapropism.

Name

WHICH ONE FITS?

In an analogy, the first pair of words must have the same relationship as the words in the second pair. To solve an analogy, look for the connection between the words in the complete pair. That relationship is the key to finding the missing word and solving the analogy!

Identify the relationship in each complete pair of words. Then find in the box the word that completes the analogy.

1. Quarrel **is to** argument **as** rubbish **is to** _____.

2. Sullen **is to** glum **as** timid **is to** _____.

3. Peril **is to** _____ **as** hectic **is to** chaotic.

4. Noisy **is to** clamorous **as** _____ **is to** splendid.

5. Minimize **is to** maximize **as** _____ **is to** expensive.

6. _____ **is to** mimic **as** impeccable **is to** faultless.

7. Friend **is to** _____ **as** enemy **is to** opponent.

8. _____ **is to** release **as** evidence **is to** conjecture.

9. Freedom **is to** slavery **as** _____ **is to** final.

10. Savory **is to** tasty **as** boring **is to** _____.

Dexter is to *me* as air is to *life*!

That's a little extreme!

WORD BOX

cheap	danger	mute
bold	ending	initial
garbage	ally	generous
superb	fun	retain
copy	greedy	shy
thrill	quiet	monotonous

Name _____

ANALOGIES AREN'T SCARY

In an analogy, the words in the first pair must have the same relationship as the words in the second pair. When you try to solve an analogy, begin by deciding what the relationship is between the two words you are given.

scary : terryifying AS _____ : freezing

What is the relationship between *scary* and *terrifying?* Terrifying is an extreme form of scary. So, in the next pair, *freezing* must be an extreme form of something. An answer such as cool would complete the analogy.

Identify the relationship for each analogy. Write the code letter at the beginning of each example (see the box). Then circle the word that best completes the analogy.

_____ 1. insolvent : rich :: penniless : _____
poor   flush   millionaire   pauper

_____ 2. mischief : violence :: _____ : insult
attack   harmless   compliment   teasing

_____ 3. squirrel : nuts :: _____ : money
wealth   wallet   spendthrift   pauper

_____ 4. pebble : _____ :: minnow : fish
gravel   rock   sand   mountain

_____ 5. blush : embarrassed :: fume : _____
smile   temper   enraged   worried

_____ 6. _____ : drip :: mitt : baseball
bat   bucket   water   catch

_____ 7. perfume : fragrant :: garbage : _____
refuse   fetid   odor   savory

_____ 8. seasoned : _____ :: inexperienced : novice
young   experienced   veteran   amateur

_____ 9. _____ : justice :: classroom : learning
criminal   lawsuits   judge   courtroom

_____ 10. projectile : _____ :: dormitory : dormant
injection   throw   sleep   proceed

Codes

S = synonym
A = antonym
C = in the same
    category
D = degree
F = function
L = location
W = word form
R = response, result,
    or action

SCRAPING CHALK : CHALKBOARD ::
SQUEAKING HINGE : DOOR

Not all analogies are scary.
Some are just bad.

Name _____

HOT AND COLD

Things are heating up in this passage. The author has chosen words to help you feel the temperatures.

Read the poem. When you find an unfamiliar word, try to determine its meaning from clues in the surrounding text. Then follow the directions below.

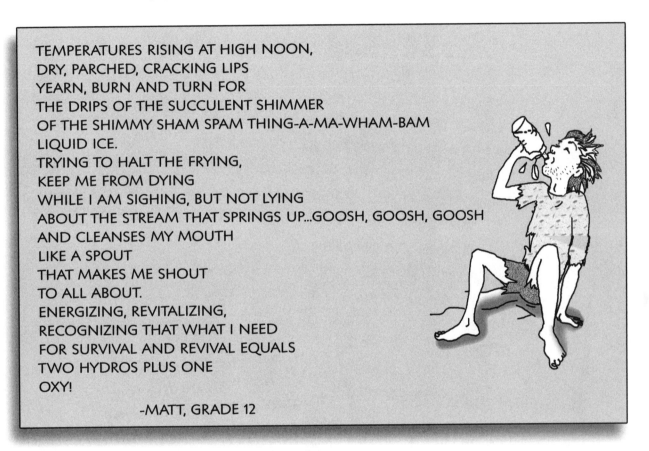

TEMPERATURES RISING AT HIGH NOON,
DRY, PARCHED, CRACKING LIPS
YEARN, BURN AND TURN FOR
THE DRIPS OF THE SUCCULENT SHIMMER
OF THE SHIMMY SHAM SPAM THING-A-MA-WHAM-BAM
LIQUID ICE.
TRYING TO HALT THE FRYING,
KEEP ME FROM DYING
WHILE I AM SIGHING, BUT NOT LYING
ABOUT THE STREAM THAT SPRINGS UP...GOOSH, GOOSH, GOOSH
AND CLEANSES MY MOUTH
LIKE A SPOUT
THAT MAKES ME SHOUT
TO ALL ABOUT.
ENERGIZING, REVITALIZING,
RECOGNIZING THAT WHAT I NEED
FOR SURVIVAL AND REVIVAL EQUALS
TWO HYDROS PLUS ONE
OXY!

-MATT, GRADE 12

1. Use the context of the poem to define these words:

   parched (line 2)–

   yearn (line 3) –

   succulent (line 4) –

   revitalizing (line 15) –

2. What is the central idea of this poem? How do you know?

Name

Common Core Reinforcement Activities — 8th Grade Language

THE CRUSH

There are many ways to tell a story. Two common structures of text are poetry and prose. Although these two selections differ in structure, they both address the same theme and offer similar messages.

As you read, notice how each structure contributes to the development of the theme. Then compare the selections on the next page (page 37).

A.

Every time the phone rings, your heart skips a beat. You have begun to absent-mindedly write senseless poetry again. Your heart feels so full that you are afraid it just might burst. Your body feels strange and incomplete. You seem to forget more than usual. You notice every red car that passes and hope it might be his. Your auditory sense has improved one hundred percent, except when you are talking to him — then you can't even understand your own words. This is how you know you have developed a crush.

-Kate, Grade 10

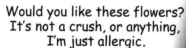
Would you like these flowers?
It's not a crush, or anything,
I'm just allergic.

B.

Love is like the sun
Shining through the fog.
If I can catch just one ray
Everything will look brighter
And I will feel warmth.
To have no love
Is to have no sun
And I am certain to perish
Without each one.
Even to love and be disappointed
Is better than to live without love,
For it is much more enjoyable
To have brief sunlight
Than none at all.

-Anonymous, Grade 9

Name

36

THE CRUSH, CONTINUED

Using the two texts on page 36, complete this diagram. In the left circle, tell how the prose text develops the theme. Refer to such aspects as tone, word choice, organization, or anything else unique to the prose. In the right circle, do the same for the poem. In the center section, note things that are common to both texts.

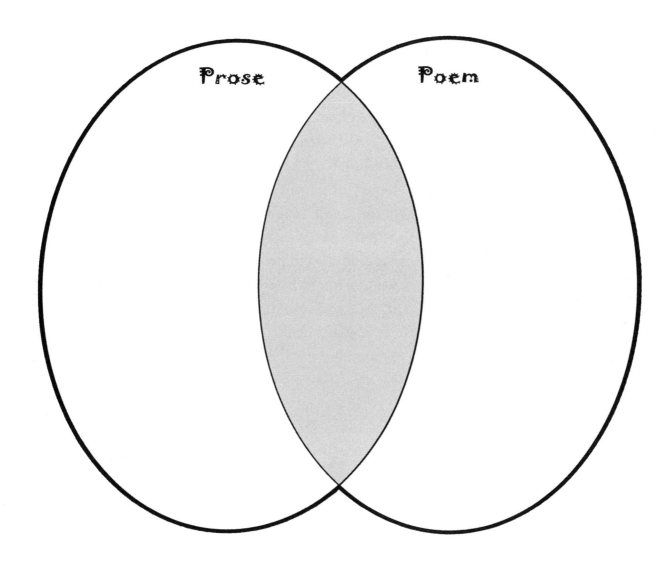

Which most effectively develops the theme? _____

Explain your choice.

Name _____

A NIGHT OF KNIGHTS

Stories of knights from medieval times have captivated audiences for thousands of years. These long-ago tales have influenced literature and other kinds of presentations up to and including the present day.

Read this brief introduction to the topic to learn how this all got started. Follow the directions below, then go on to the passage and questions on page 39.

The Round Table was the table at which King Arthur, the legendary British ruler, sat with his knights. The term Round Table also refers to Arthur's entire royal court. The first mention of the round table was in a story dated 1155. The story tells how Arthur decided to seat his knights around a circular table so they wouldn't fight over who sat in places of honor. In medieval literature, knights considered membership at the Round Table a great honor. Brave men came to Arthur's court from many countries hoping to be chosen a member.

Work consulted:
"Round Table." *World Book Online Reference Center.* World Book, 2013. Web. 9 Oct. 2013.

1. Join with two or three other students to brainstorm modern examples (such as books, movies, dramas, television shows, or video games) that include King Arthur and/or knights. Write your ideas below:

2. Why do you think the idea of the brave knight is so popular?

Name

Use with page 39.

38

A NIGHT OF KNIGHTS, CONTINUED

One modern example of a story about knights can be found in Mark Twain's novel
A Connecticut Yankee in King Arthur's Court. In it, a man is transported from the late 1800s
back in time to the 500s. Here is part of the man's description of what he sees:

Read the passage and answer the questions that follow.

"In the middle of this…vaulted public square was an oaken table which they called the Table Round. It was as large as a circus ring; and around it sat a great company of men dressed in such various and splendid colors that it hurt one's eyes to look at them. They wore their plumed hats, right along, except that whenever one addressed himself directly to the king, he lifted his hat a trifle just as he was beginning his remark."

"Mainly the Round Table talk was monologues—narrative accounts of the adventures in which these prisoners were captured and their friends and backers killed and stripped of their steeds and armor. As a general thing—as far as I could make out—these murderous adventures were not forays undertaken to avenge injuries, nor to settle old disputes or sudden fallings out; no, as a rule they were simply duels between strangers—duels between people who had never even been introduced to each other, and between whom existed no cause of offense whatever.

Work cited:
Twain, Mark. *A Connecticut Yankee in King Arthur's Court.* New York: Harper and Bros, 1889.
Google Books. Web. 7 Nov. 2013.

3. How does the narrator's point of view add humor to the story?

4. This story is also one of the first examples of an author writing about time travel. List some more recent stories (such as books, movies, dramas, television shows, or video games)) that also use time travel as part of their plots:

Use with page 38.

Name

SLOW AND STEADY

This may be one of the most well-known races in history! It's a traditional story that has been told again and again across many generations. Sometimes the themes, characters, or events from such traditional stories appear in new and unique ways in other stories.

Read this translation of "The Tortoise and the Hare," one of Aesop's fables. Think of other places you have heard stories similar to this one.

A Hare one day ridiculed the short feet and slow pace of the Tortoise. The latter, laughing, said: "Though you be swift as the wind, I will beat you in a race." The Hare, deeming her assertion to be simply impossible, assented to the proposal; and they agreed that the Fox should choose the course, and fix the goal. On the day appointed for the race, they started together. The Tortoise never for a moment stopped, but went on with a slow but steady pace straight to the end of the course. The Hare, trusting to his native swiftness, cared little about the race, and laying down by the wayside, fell fast asleep. At last waking up, and moving as fast as he could, he saw the Tortoise had reached the goal, and was comfortably dozing after her fatigue.

I can't stop laughing!

Work cited:
Aesop. "The Hare and the Tortoise." Trans. George Fyler Townsend. *Three Hundred and Fifty Aesop's Fables: Literally Translated from the Greek*. Chicago: Belford, Clarke & Co., 1885. 43-44. Print.

Restate the moral (lesson) of this story in your own words:	List books, television shows, or movies that have a message similar to that of this fable:

Name

THE DILEMMA

In the story of Jada's dilemma, the characters involved have different views of the situation. Jada herself has more than one! Points of view play a key role in developing a story.

Identify the point of view of each character. Be ready to discuss the evidence from the text that led to your answers.

Jada is struggling with a conflict. This problem is trickier than most because it involves her parents AND a teacher! She's not sure she will ever be able to decide what to do; but she has to—and soon.

I'm so upset about the grade I got on that science test! Mr. Lucas didn't grade it fairly. I DO understand plant processes; he just didn't read my answers carefully. I tried to talk to him, but he was too closed-minded! He said the grade could not be changed. I never should have said anything to my mom!

. . . and now my parents are all worked up about this low grade . . . They know how hard I studied. They are going to call the school in the morning and make an appointment to see Mr. Lucas.

. . . and then what? Mr. Lucas will think I'm a big baby getting my parents to fix things for me. This will only make matters worse. From now on, he'll be even harder on me. I just know he'll hold a grudge. Teachers don't like to be challenged by parents. I should have pushed harder for him to reconsider my grade.

. . . but I can't live with this grade when I know I don't deserve it! My grade-point average will be ruined, and it's not a true picture of my work in science class. I don't want a bad grade, but I don't want my parents showing up at school to rescue me, either.

Jada's points of view:

Teacher's point of view:

Parent's point of view:

Name

A DIFFERENT LOOK

When you enjoy a story in more than one format, you get more adventure, mystery, entertainment, or fun! Many works of literature (poems, plays, novels, etc.) have been remade into films or other presentations. Use this form to compare and contrast a written and a visual version of the same story.

Choose a book that you have read or that is easily available—one that has a movie version. Your school or public librarian can help. Read or review the book. Watch or re-watch the movie. Sharpen your attention to compare elements of the story presented in the two forms.

	Written Version	Film Version
Title of the work		
Major characters		
Setting(s)		
Theme(s) or message(s)		

1. What, if any, major differences did you notice in the storylines of the two versions?

2. What visual techniques did the filmmaker use to enhance the story?

3. What sounds added to the film version of the story?

4. If a friend could experience only one version of the story, which one would you tell him or her to choose? Explain your reasons.

Name

READING

INFORMATIONAL TEXT

Grade 8

JUMP!

Understanding nonfiction requires many of the same skills needed to read fiction. Such strategies as paraphrasing, summarizing, asking questions, and picturing images in your mind will help you understand and remember what you read. You should also be able to point to evidence in the text to confirm your conclusions about the text.

Read this writer's opinion about bungee jumping; then answer the questions in the boxes. Be ready to discuss your opinions (and reasons) about participation in this sport.

Bungee jumping is a sport that combines the thrill and danger of free fall with the assurance that the elastic cord will save you from disaster. The first bungee jumpers were called land divers; they jumped from trees, towers, or cliffs with vines tied to their legs. Early U.S. bungee jumpers mostly jumped from bridges. Now people around the world also jump from platforms, cliffs, helicopters, balloons, and other high places. Great attention came to bungee jumping in 1987 when a man named A. J. Hackett jumped from the Eiffel Tower!

Some argue that there is a greater chance of being injured or killed in a car accident than of being injured or killed while bungee jumping—that when all procedures are followed, the bungee cord stops a fall just as safely as the brakes stop a moving car. There are, however, reports of injuries to the eyes and limbs caused by the shock of the abrupt stop at the end of the cord. Most other injuries and deaths have been caused by the jumper's error, lack of safety precautions, or factors beyond the jumper's control.

SAFE?
What evidence supports the idea that the sport is safe?

UNSAFE?
What evidence supports the idea that the sport is dangerous?

Works consulted:
"Eiffel Tower." *ajhackett.com.* AJ Hackett Int., 2013. Web. 3 Nov. 2013.
"Safety." *bungee.ie* The Irish Bungee Jumping Company, 2013. Web. 3 Nov. 2013.

Name

SERIOUS SURFING

When you watch a skilled surfer ride a wave, the sport may seem like effortless fun. Not so—surfers need to understand how the waves work and how to ride them safely and successfully. Here's a small sample of some information surfers may know.

Read all the texts below, then complete items 1-5.

Wave Hydrodynamics

One factor that determines wave shape is the topography (geographic features) of the seabed directly behind and immediately beneath a breaking wave. The upthrust of the wave is proportional to the incline of the seabed. When a swell (building wave) passes over a sudden steep slope, the force of the upthrust causes the top of the wave (the curl) to be thrown forward, forming a curtain of water that plunges to the wave trough below. The ocean-bottom or shore topography in front of a swell helps determine how long the breaking wave lasts. When a swell runs along a slope, it continues to peel (break over time) for as long as that slope lasts. When a swell runs into a bay or an island, the breaking wave diminishes in size as the wave front fans out.

The Surfrider Foundation is a nonprofit organization dedicated to the protection and preservation of the world's oceans, waves, and beaches. It was founded in 1984 by a small group of surfers and now has thousands of members.

Works consulted:
"Surf Terms." *Surfing–Waves,* Surfing–Waves.com, n.d. Web. 1 Nov. 2013.
    Web. 3 Nov. 2013.
Surfrider Foundation. Web. 3 Nov. 2013.
"What Makes a Wave Break, Peel, or Close Out?" *Surfing News Daily. N.p.,*
    29 Mar. 2012. Web. 3 Nov. 2013.

1. What is the purpose of the Surfrider Foundation?

2. Circle the maneuver that is not proper surfing etiquette.

   snap   **goofy foot**   **pearl**   **drop in on**

3. Is the following statement true or false? _____

   The topography behind, under, and in front of a swell helps to determine the shape of the resulting breaking wave as well as its duration.

On the back of this paper:

4. Write a short sentence to explain how the steepness of an incline under a developing wave affects its upthrust.

5. Draw a diagram of a breaking wave passing over a sudden steep slope. Label the **wave trough** and the **curl.** Draw an arrow to show the direction of the upthrust.

Common Surf Terms

DROP IN - dropping into or engaging a wave

DROP IN ON - taking off on a wave in front of someone closer to the wave's peak (considered inappropriate surfing behavior)

GOOFY FOOT - left foot on the back of the board

NATURAL FOOT - right foot on the back of the board

PEARL - accidentally driving the nose of the board underwater, generally ending the ride

SNAP - a quick, sharp turn off the top of a wave

Name

LOOSE WITH THE FACTS

When reading informational texts, it is important to distinguish fact from opinion. A *fact* is something true that can be tested or proven. An *opinion* is someone's belief or judgment.

This writer has been a bit loose with the facts. As you read the information about Hawaii (written as a "factual" report by a young visitor to the state), focus on distinguishing provable facts from opinions.

Hawaii is the newest of the fifty United States and is the most beautiful state of all. It is made of 132 islands, extending 1,523 miles (2,451 kilometers) in length. It is the only state in the union completely surrounded by water. No wonder it is the favorite playground of mainland Americans! Miles of beaches and warm surf, moderate temperatures, long hours of sunshine, beautiful sunsets, and brilliantly colored flowers that bloom year round have made this state a tourist spot sought out by people from all over the world.

Some key products of Hawaii are pineapple, sugar cane, tropical fruits, coffee, macadamia nuts, and fish. Recreation and tourism are the main sources of income for many islanders. The first settlers to Hawaii brought much of their Polynesian tradition to the islands. Their dances (including the hula), religions, chants, and customs are the main source of the beauty and richness of island life. Over the years, new arrivals have come to seek their fortunes, build homes, and raise families, so the culture has taken on additional facets and flavors. Modern Hawaii is a wonderful mixture of different cultures, making it a fascinating place to live and a delightful place to vacation.

Work consulted:
Boylan, Dan, and Lyndon Wester. "Hawaii." *World Book Student.* World Book, 2013. Web. 24 Nov. 2013.
© World Book, Inc. Reprinted with permission. All rights reserved.

In the first column, write phrases that are facts. In the center column, write phrases that are opinions. In the final column, give a reason for each choice.

Facts	Opinions	Reason

Name

GONE BANANAS

Informational text is not always in paragraphs or essays. It can come in many forms. This information is presented as an advertisement for a record-setting dessert.

Read the poster carefully. Then answer the questions.

Come See the World's Longest Banana Split

4.55 miles long   Stretches the length of the town along Market Street

2,500 gallons of ice cream (6,000 scoops)

33,000 fresh, sliced bananas

24,000 soft red maraschino cherries

600 pounds of chopped nuts

450 gallons of topping

A DELIGHT OF ICY CREAM DRIZZLED WITH STREAMS OF CHOCOLATE SAUCE, PROUDLY WEARING PUFFY HATS OF SWEET MARSHMALLOW CREAM, SPRINKLED WITH NUTS, DECORATED WITH PLUMP, MOUTHWATERING CHERRIES

Made with loving care by the residents of Selinsgrove, Pennsylvania, for a high school fundraiser April 30, 1988

Sorry, only one spoonful for each visitor!

1. What is the main idea of this selection?

2. How can you tell the main idea?

3. Who is the intended audience?

4. What is the purpose of the poster?

5. Circle four words from the selection that would be convincing to help accomplish the purpose. What else helps accomplish the purpose?

Works consulted:

Simpson, Jenna. "Event Commemorates Largest Banana Split." *The Crusader Online.* Susquehanna University, 12 Sept. 2003. Web. 2 Nov. 2013.

"World's Longest Banana Split History." *worldslongestbananasplit.com.* World's Longest Banana Split, n.d. Web. 2 Nov. 2013.

Name

TARANTULA TALK

Tarantulas—are they as terrifying as many people think? This encyclopedia article may shed some light on the question.

Any time you research a topic, you will need to be able to analyze and summarize reference materials. As you read this text, notice how its organization contributes to the communication of its main and supporting ideas.

Tarantula

Tarantula is a common name for a family of mostly large spiders. Tarantulas inhabit warm climates around the world, especially tropical regions. Some types live for more than 20 years. Tarantulas get their name from a distantly related wolf spider that lives around Taranto in Italy. People once believed this spider's bite caused a disease called tarantism. The victims supposedly leaped in the air and ran about making strange noises. According to superstition, the best cure was a lively Italian folk dance that became known as the tarantella.

Many tarantulas live in burrows, and a few inhabit trees. Some types have a poisonous bite that can prove harmful to people. Most tarantulas, however, are not particularly poisonous. Their chief means of defense consists of thousands of tiny, irritating, hairlike body parts that can be flung into the air by rubbing motions of the hind legs.

Work cited:
"Tarantula." *World Book Online Reference Center.* World Book, 2013. Web. 11 Oct. 2013.
© World Book, Inc. Reprinted with permission. All rights reserved.

Now use the diagram on the next page (page 49) as you closely examine the text to identify key ideas and supporting details.

Name

TARANTULA TALK, CONTINUED

Fill in each unshaded rectangle with a detail from the text that supports a key idea.

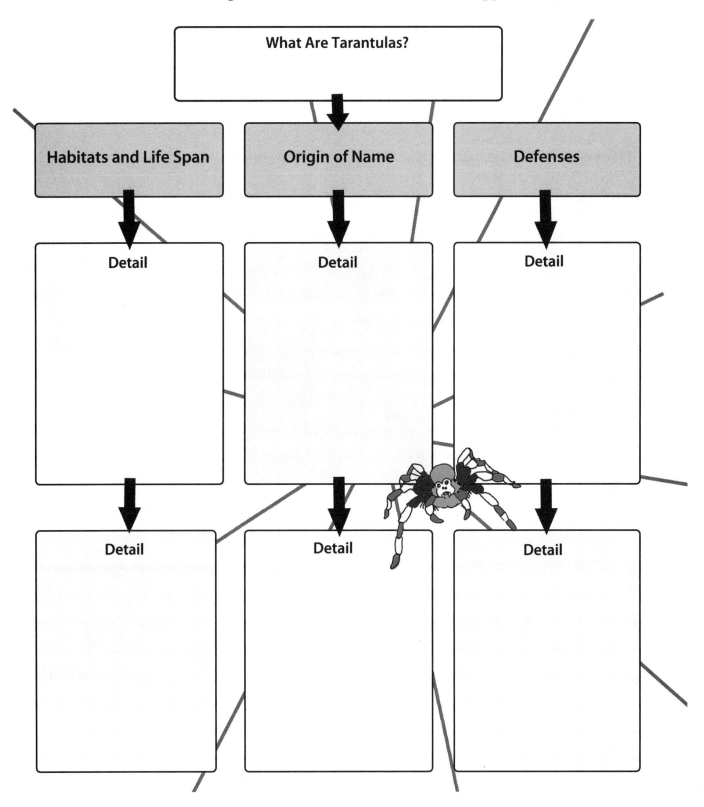

What Are Tarantulas?

Habitats and Life Span

Origin of Name

Defenses

Detail

Detail

Detail

Detail

Detail

Detail

BEN FRANKLIN'S PLAN

On a long voyage, Benjamin Franklin, one of the Founding Fathers of the United States, decided to make a plan to improve himself and his life. Below is an excerpt from his autobiography where he tells about this endeavor.

To summarize means to identify and concisely re-tell the most important ideas in a text. Being able to summarize, both during and after reading, will help you remember information more easily. Read this excerpt to find out about Ben's plan. Answer the questions below the passage.

It was about this time I conceived the bold and arduous project of arriving at moral perfection. I wished to live without committing any fault at any time; I would conquer all that either natural inclination, custom, or company might lead me into. As I knew, or thought I knew, what was right and wrong, I did not see why I might not always do the one and avoid the other. But I soon found I had undertaken a task of more difficulty than I had imagined. While my care was employed in guarding against one fault, I was often surprised by another; habit took the advantage of inattention; inclination was sometimes too strong for reason. I concluded, at length, that the mere conviction that it was our interest to be completely virtuous was not sufficient to prevent our slipping; and that the contrary habits must be broken, and good ones acquired and established, before we can have any dependence on a steady, uniform rectitude of conduct.

Work cited:
Franklin, Benjamin. *The Autobiography of Benjamin Franklin*. Boston: Houghton, Mifflin and Co., 1888. *Google Books*. Web. 7 Nov. 2013.

1. What is Franklin trying to achieve?

2. What makes him think this is possible?

3. What gets in his way?

4. What does he decide he has to do to reach his goal?

Now summarize this selection in exactly 25 words (one word on each line).

_____ _____ _____ _____ _____

_____ _____ _____ _____ _____

_____ _____ _____ _____ _____

Name

START WITH A PLATEAU

Three landforms have a close connection. This essay will spell it out.

Complete the diagram to show the relationships between the three landforms.

It's all about the flat top. Then again, it's all about the steep sides. And yet again, it's all about the size. Remember all these factors to understand these three landforms: a *plateau,* a *mesa,* and a *butte.*

All three landforms share some features. They are high, layered rock areas with steep sides that rise up abruptly from lower land around them. Unlike hills or mountains, these landforms have flat tops.

A *plateau* is the largest. It is a huge, flat, high, broad area with at least one side that rises sharply. A plateau is not as high as a mountain. Many *plateaus* cover hundreds or thousands of square miles. A mesa is smaller than a *plateau,* but can still cover many square miles and rise hundreds of feet high. It is sometimes called tableland or a flat-topped hill. A butte is smaller than a mesa and has no vegetation. Mesas and buttes are common in the deserts and plains of the southwestern United States.

Buttes, mesas, and *plateaus* have a very close relationship. Every *butte* forms from a *mesa,* which forms from a *plateau.* When softer layers of rock in a plateau are worn away by erosion, a *mesa* is the result. A *butte* is the last stage in the process, because it is the rock that remains when some of the *mesa* is eroded away. To remember these three formations, just remember to start with a *plateau* and add erosion.

- by Lowell, grade 7

Name

Common Core Reinforcement Activities — 8th Grade Language

DRESS CODE DISSENSION

The topic of a dress code stirs up plenty of discussion (and often plenty of dissension, too) in many schools. Mt. Stensen Middle School was no exception. Over the summer, a committee of teachers and administrators created a proposal for a new student dress code.

Parents were asked to review the proposal and respond with notes or emails. Some of those were posted, along with the proposed dress code, on the bulletin board shown on the next page (page 53).

Use the dress code text on page 53 as you follow these directions.

1. Scan the notes on the bulletin board. What do you notice right away about the nature of the comments?

2. Read all the text closely. How does the structure of the Proposed Dress Code text affect the writer's message or purpose?

3. Look at the bulletin board as a whole. How does the combination of text forms work together to speak to the topic of "Dress Code Dissension"?

4. Examine the cartoon. What does this add to the text as a whole?

5. Find the following words in the text. Use the context of the text to arrive at a definition of each word.

a. proposed

b. violated

c. restrictive

d. assure

e. discrimination

f. affluent

I'm actually okay with a dress code.

Name

DRESS CODE DISSENSION, CONTINUED

Mt. Stensen Middle School
Proposed DRESS CODE

- No T-shirts, muscle shirts, or athletic shirts
- No visible underwear or midriffs
- No gang-related garments, words, or symbols
- No open-toed shoes or sandals
- No jeans or denim clothing
- No shorts
- No bedroom slippers or pajamas
- No hooded sweatshirts or hats
- No sagging pants
- No spaghetti straps, backless, low-cut, strapless or halter-style tops or dresses
- Boys: Shirts must have collars, and must be tucked into pants at all times.
- Girls: Skirts or dresses must reach below the length of the fingertips when arms are straight down at sides.

I feel that my daughter's personal style and individual rights are violated by this dress code. It is far too restrictive.
- Dr. Ronald Zimmer

Kids will still find ways to bend these rules. It's time for uniforms. They will assure appropriate dress and eliminate clothing competitions.
- Mrs. Judith McGraw

WE WANT UNIFORMS

Finally! It's good to see you requiring students to dress decently!
-Susan Jackson

What dress code?

OUR FAMILY CANNOT AFFORD TO BUY ONE WHOLE SET OF CLOTHING FOR SCHOOL AND ANOTHER FOR OUTSIDE SCHOOL—FOR THREE CHILDREN. STUDENTS WILL NOT WANT TO WEAR THESE "DRESS CODE" CLOTHES ANYWHERE BUT SCHOOL. THIS FEELS LIKE DISCRIMINATION AGAINST LESS AFFLUENT FAMILIES.
-ANTHONY MOSCHEO

Name _____

TAKING OFFICE

On January 20, 1961, President John F. Kennedy became the 35th president of the United States and delivered his inaugural address.

As you read this excerpt from Kennedy's speech, notice his choice of words and their impact on the meaning and tone of the speech.

Let the word go forth from this time and place, to friend and foe alike, that the torch has been passed to a new generation of Americans—born in this century, tempered by war, disciplined by a hard and bitter peace, proud of our ancient heritage—and unwilling to witness or permit the slow undoing of those human rights to which this Nation has always been committed, and to which we are committed today at home and around the world.

Let every nation know, whether it wishes us well or ill, that we shall pay any price, bear any burden, meet any hardship, support any friend, oppose any foe, in order to assure the survival and the success of liberty.

Work cited:
Kennedy, John F. "Inaugural Address - January 20, 1961." *The American Presidency Project*. The American Presidency Project, 2013. Web. 7. Nov. 2013.

1. Explain the meaning of each word in the context of the speech.

   a. foe-

   b. heritage -

   c. burden-

   d. assure-

2. What is the tone of this speech? Explain your answer.

3. What impact does Kennedy's word choice have on the message of the second paragraph? Explain your answer.

Name

HOW GRAND!

This paragraph describing the Grand Canyon is taken from a text published in 1912. Some of the vocabulary words are probably unfamiliar to modern readers, but many of them can be understood by paying close attention to both the tone and structure of the piece.

Read the passage closely. Then answer the questions below.

And the principal member of this great system (of canyons) has been named The Grand Canyon, as a conscious and meaningful tribute to its vastness, its sublimity, its grandeur and its awesomeness. It is unique; it stands alone. Though only two hundred and seventeen miles long, it expresses within that distance more than any one human mind yet has been able to comprehend or interpret to the world. Famous word-masters have attempted it; great canvas and colormasters have tried it; but all alike have failed. It is one of the few things that man is utterly unable to imagine until he comes in actual contact with it. A strange being, a strange [6]ower, an unknown reptile, a unique machine, or a strange and unknown anything, almost, within the ken of man, can be explained to another so that he will reasonably comprehend it; but not so with the Grand Canyon.

Work cited:
James, George W. *The Grand Canyon of Arizona*. Boston: Little, Brown, and Co., 1912.
Google Books. Web. 7 Nov. 2013.

1. What is the tone of this description? (Tone is the attitude of the writer toward the topic, or how the author feels about the topic.)

2. How is the tone reflected in the word choice?

3. Here are some of the words the author uses to describe the Grand Canyon:

   vastness, sublimity, grandeur, awesomeness, unique

   Even if you don't know what all of these words mean, what can you infer about them based on the paragraph?

4. Re-read the last sentence. Given its context, what do you think "within the ken of man" means?

Name

FOOD-FIGHT FRENZY

According to the McCuffy Middle School newspaper, last Wednesday was an eventful day at the school. A newspaper page generally presents informational text in a report form. But sometimes, the newspaper will print further reports, related information, or opinions about an event. This newspaper has all of these.

Read all the sections of the front page of *The Bull Horn*, found on the next page, page 57.

1. How many different points of view on the incident were evident on this page? (Describe each one. Name the person or persons and describe each viewpoint.)

2. What did the sidebar article ("27 Students Face Detention") provide that was not a part of the main article about the food fight?

3. What did the cartoon add to the overall effect of the text?

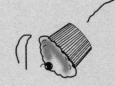

4. What is the meaning of the phrase "allegedly started the fracas" in the first paragraph of the main article?

5. What is the meaning of the word "missiles" in the third paragraph of the main story?

6. What did Principal Whimple mean when he said, "Steps are being taken"?

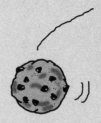

Name _____

Use with page 57.

The Bull Horn

McCuffy Middle School

March 4, this year   *Volume 8, Number 11*

Flying Soda Can Sends One Student to the Hospital

27 Students Face Detention

Students who were identified as being actively involved in Wednesday's food fight will spend the next five Saturdays cleaning and repainting the school cafeteria. Damages, including broken glass and furniture, will be paid for from the seventh and eighth grade end-of-year party fund. The students involved will also write apologies to their fellow students, the faculty, and the cafeteria workers. Each apology must bear the signature of a parent or guardian.

Last Wednesday during lunch, the school cafeteria erupted in a food- fight frenzy. Seventh-grader Tess Nellson allegedly started the fracas when she grabbed a piece of lemon crème pie and smacked it into eighth-grader Roger Boyle's face. The place went nuts! Soon, dozens got into the act, and the food really started flying!

Rollicking students, drenched in Italian dressing, French fries, Spanish rice, Canadian bacon, and American cheese, cheerfully bombarded each other with any edible substance they could find.

Orin Peeples slid halfway across the room on a banana peel. Missiles of mush peppered the walls. The scene turned ugly, however, when someone started throwing full cans of soda. By the time teachers and administrators arrived with school security, at least one student had been injured.

Tess Nellson was beaned with a soda can and was taken to the emergency room for five stitches.

When we interviewed Principal Whimple about the incident, he told us, "Steps are being taken." He plans to address the student body on Friday about the incident.

Comment Corner

Students who witnessed the famous food fight had this to say:

"Man, oh man, it was crazy. I've never had so much fun!"
   – Ed Whelp, 8th grade

"Someone dumped spaghetti sauce over my new High School Rocks T-shirt, and it's ruined. I'm really bummed."
         – Lisa Grummel,
            6th grade

"I got some great photos with my cellphone. I think I'll sell them to the city newspaper."
      – Dorothy Braidy,
         8th grade

"It was scary. Some of the students were out of control. It felt like a mob!"
         – Ivan Shue,
            7th grade

Food flew and chaos ruled during last Wednesday's furious food fight.

(Photo by Dorothy Braidy)

Name   Use with page 56.

A FAMOUS ADDRESS

One of the most famous presidential speeches ever delivered came to be known as the "Gettysburg Address." U.S. President Abraham Lincoln gave this speech in 1863 at a ceremony to dedicate a portion of a battlefield as a cemetery for those who had lost their lives in the Civil War.

Lincoln had a very specific purpose in mind when he gave this short speech. As you read it, see if you can identify his argument and the evidence he gives to support it. Then answer the questions on the next page (page 59).

Four score and seven years ago our fathers brought forth on this continent, a new nation, conceived in Liberty, and dedicated to the proposition that all men are created equal.

Now we are engaged in a great civil war, testing whether that nation, or any nation so conceived and so dedicated, can long endure. We are met on a great battle-field of that war. We have come to dedicate a portion of that field, as a final resting place for those who here gave their lives that that nation might live. It is altogether fitting and proper that we should do this.

But, in a larger sense, we can not dedicate — we can not consecrate — we can not hallow — this ground. The brave men, living and dead, who struggled here, have consecrated it, far above our poor power to add or detract. The world will little note, nor long remember what we say here, but it can never forget what they did here. It is for us the living, rather, to be dedicated here to the unfinished work which they who fought here have thus far so nobly advanced. It is rather for us to be here dedicated to the great task remaining before us — that from these honored dead we take increased devotion to that cause for which they gave the last full measure of devotion — that we here highly resolve that these dead shall not have died in vain — that this nation, under God, shall have a new birth of freedom — and that government of the people, by the people, for the people, shall not perish from the earth.

Work cited:
Lincoln, Abraham. "Gettysburg Address." 1863. *World Book Online Reference Center.* World Book, 2013. Web. 10 Oct. 2013. © World Book, Inc. Reprinted with permission. All rights reserved.

Name

Use with page 59.

A FAMOUS ADDRESS, CONTINUED

After a close reading of the "Gettysburg Address," complete these:

1. To help you analyze the text of Lincoln's speech, look up the following words and write a definition for each:

   dedicate -

   consecrate -

   hallow -

   resolve -

   perish -

2. Lincoln began the speech by reminding the crowd of the foundations of America. To what does this refer?

3. In the second section, he argues, "we cannot …consecrate…" the battlefield. Why not?

4. What is the purpose of this speech? Explain your answer.

5. Why has this become one of the most famous speeches ever delivered? Explain the reasons for your answer.

Use with page 58.

Name

A QUESTION OF SAGGING

Many nonfiction selections are written with the purpose of expressing an opinion or making an argument for an idea. Good argumentative writing gives evidence, facts, and examples to support a main claim.

Read this argumentative essay. Then use the organizer on the next page (page 61) to summarize and evaluate the argument.

Pull Up Your Pants!!

Collaboration by an 8th Grade Class

Being fashionable is one thing. Showing your underwear (or backside!) in school is another. Within reason, people should have the right to dress the way they like, but there are limits to what is okay for school. The wearing of baggy pants (sometimes called "sagging") is completely inappropriate and should be banned in all schools.

First, wearing baggy pants can be a safety hazard. Pants that are way below the waist are usually much too long also (because they're pulled down). Students can step on their own or others' hems, and that will result in tripping. Tripping and falling in a crowd or on stairs could also endanger other students.

Next, sagging is disrespectful. Because the trend is said to have started in the prison culture, it makes law breaking seem like a thing to be admired. Sagging is also a form of indecency, and indecency is outlawed in states across America. In fact, several places, including counties in Louisiana, Florida, Illinois, and New York, have outlawed baggy pants in particular.

Finally, sagging does not belong in a school setting because it's distracting. Schools are for learning, and students (and teachers) need the chance to concentrate on learning without having to look at people's underwear or private parts. In middle schools and high schools, teenagers (with teen hormones in full force) have enough trouble focusing without those distractions! Some schools even require uniforms for all students, and one of the reasons often cited is that uniforms get rid of the distractions that some clothing can bring.

Self-expression is fine. Self-expression to the point of being disrespectful, hazardous, or distracting is not fine. Students need to pull up their pants and find safe and respectful ways to show their individuality. Sagging should be banned!

Works consulted:
Carbone, Nick. "Floridians, Hike Up Your Pants: It's the Law." *Time Newsfeed*. Time, 8 May 2011. Web. 10 Nov. 2013.
Koppel, Niko. "Are Your Jeans Sagging? Go Directly to Jail." *The New York TImes*. The New York Times, 30 Aug. 2007. Web. 10 Nov. 2013.
Lauren, Leibowitz. "Baggy Pants Law Will Fine Offenders in Louisiana Parish." *Huffington Post Style*. TheHuffingtonPost.com, 17 Apr. 2013. Web. 10 Nov. 2013.
Trice, Dawn. "What Do Baggy Pants Really Say?" *Chicago Tribune*. Chicago Tribune, 2 Nov. 2009. Web. 10 Nov. 2013.

Name

Use with page 61.

A QUESTION OF SAGGING, CONTINUED

Complete this organizer to analyze the argument on page 60.

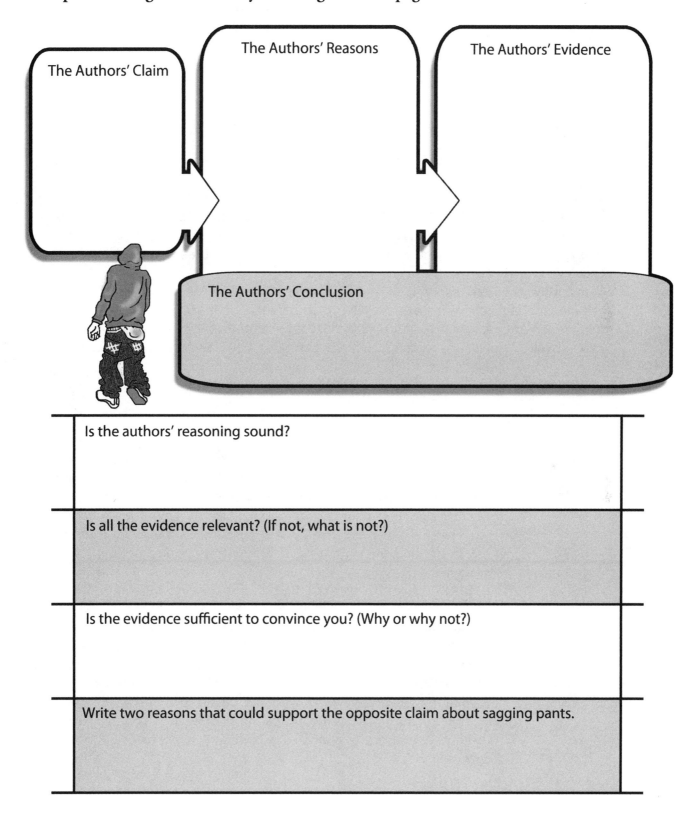

The Authors' Claim

The Authors' Reasons

The Authors' Evidence

The Authors' Conclusion

Is the authors' reasoning sound?

Is all the evidence relevant? (If not, what is not?)

Is the evidence sufficient to convince you? (Why or why not?)

Write two reasons that could support the opposite claim about sagging pants.

Name

Use with page 60.

Common Core Reinforcement Activities — 8th Grade Language

IT'S A UFO! (OR IS IT?)

When reading informational text, you may encounter conflicting information. When that happens, it is important that you distinguish between facts and interpretations so that you can make an objective analysis of what is said.

Read these two passages about UFO's. Be prepared to discuss them when you're finished.

1 Unidentified flying object (UFO) is a light or object in the air that has no obvious explanation. Some people believe UFO's are spaceships from other planets. However, investigators discover ordinary explanations for most UFO sightings, largely because most witnesses are generally reliable individuals. UFO hoaxes are rare.

Many reported UFO's are actually bright planets, stars, or meteors. People have reported aircraft, missiles, satellites, birds, insect swarms, and weather balloons as UFO's. Unusual weather conditions also can create optical illusions that are reported as UFO's.

Investigators can explain all but a small percentage of UFO reports. The remainder may be due to an unknown phenomenon or merely to limitations in human perception, memory, and research. Most scientists believe that there is not enough reliable evidence to connect these sightings with life from other planets.

Work cited:
Oberg, James. "Unidentified flying object (UFO)." *World Book Online Reference Center.* World Book, 2013. Web. 10 Oct. 2013.

2 The year was 1947. Airline pilot Kenneth Arnold was flying over Washington state when he saw them: a group of bright objects, shaped like saucers, flying near his plane. The objects were traveling much faster than anything man-made had flown before. Pilot Arnold reported his experience to the U.S. military, who took interest in this "UFO" sighting out of both scientific curiosity and national security concerns.

In 1962, another strange occurrence was documented in a letter sent to NASA. The writer reported a "very brightly glowing object, fairly well above the Eastern horizon." The writer went on to say that "It is the opinion of both (my companion) and myself that the object behaved so much unlike conventional aircraft, that it is doubtful whether the object was conceived anywhere on this planet."

Today there are several websites where people can report UFO sightings, and more than a thousand people each year do just that. Could these all be explained by ordinary phenomena? Or do you believe in UFO's?

Work consulted:
"Close Encounters with the Fourth Dimension." *World Book Online Reference Center.* World Book, 2013. Web. 10 Oct. 2013.

Use with page 63.

Name

IT'S A UFO! (OR IS IT?), CONTINUED

Complete this organizer to analyze and evaluate the articles on page 62.

Summarize article #1 in 20 words or or fewer.	Summarize article #2 in 20 words or or fewer.

List three FACTS from article #1.	List three FACTS from article #2.

Write one OPINION from article #1.	Write one OPINION from article #2.

How do the two articles differ in overall effect?

Name

Use with page 62.

Common Core Reinforcement Activities — 8th Grade Language

THE FAMOUS DREAM

When you listen to someone deliver a speech, you actually hear (and sometimes, see) two things: **the content** (the information in the speech) and **the delivery** (how the information is said). In this activity, you will compare the content of a speech as you read it on the page with the experience of hearing the same words delivered by the writer. Look for ways that each affects you differently.

On August 28, 1963, Martin Luther King, Jr. delivered a speech to a crowd of thousands. The occasion was the March on Washington, a demonstration to promote passage of a civil rights bill and employment of African American workers. This speech has become one of the most famous of the 1900s; after reading and listening to it, see if you can figure out why.

First, find and read the text of the speech online and answer these questions:

1. What is the theme (message) of this speech?

2. What literary tools (similes, metaphors, etc.) does King use to enhance his message?

3. What parts of the speech stand out to you in its written form?

Next, watch the speech as it was broadcast on national television at the time (also available online); then answer these questions:

4. What does King do to emphasize a particular point in this speech?

5. What do you notice about King's voice as the speech progresses?

6. What parts of the speech stand out to you in this form?

7. What is the impact of this speech on you, the reader/listener?

Name

WRITING

Grade 8

LET ME CONVINCE YOU

The word "argument" might make you think of a dispute between two people, where each is trying to persuade the other that his or her point of view is the right one. Argumentative writing has some characteristics similar to such a dispute: there are usually two points of view; there are facts, reasons, and examples to support each one; and the goal is to convince the audience that your point of view is the correct one.

**Read this argument and ask yourself, "Am I convinced? Why or why not?"
Then use the next two pages to plan and write your own argument.**

Rethinking Homework

by Sara, Grade 10

An adult workday is eight hours. The workday for a high school student, especially one who is conscientious, often exceeds that by two or more hours. Why should 14- to 17-year-olds bear heavier workloads than working adults? I will argue that they shouldn't—that, for their health and well being, high school students should have less homework.

Recently I surveyed 50 students from my high school and neighboring schools. On average, students report three hours of homework each school night—about 45 minutes per class. Often it is an hour or more for each class. In addition, they put in several hours each weekend on long-term assignments or test preparation. Many students take part in after-school sports, clubs, or jobs (and teens are encouraged to participate in such things). This uses the hours in the afternoon or into the evening, leaving few hours for cramming in studies. For many students (such as myself) this adds up to a 12-hour day that begins before dawn with a long bus ride and ends with a return home after dark. And then the two or three hours of homework begin.

A 2005 study by the National Sleep Foundation claims that teenagers need eight to nine hours of sleep a night, and that only 20% of American teenagers get adequate sleep. According to the American Academy of Pediatrics, lack of adequate sleep contributes to poor attendance, lack of attention in school, decreased memory retention, unsafe driving, depressed mood, illnesses, and a risk of sports injuries.

In addition to fostering sleep deprivation, the workload robs teens of time to relax, socialize with friends, and do activities with families. In other words, it robs them of some of what being a teenager is all about. It adds stress to their lives and tension to their homes.

Eliminating homework is not the solution. I propose a reasonable workload for teenagers. Teachers could teach as much as they can in class and use some of the 250 minutes or more a week of time given to each class for students to do much of their work in class. After all, learning should be done in school in the presence of the teacher. Teachers must recognize that teens need time to live a little; they need to think about the effects of a 12- to 15-hour workday on health and learning.

With a lighter homework load, teens will get some relief from the stress of their lives. With a sane workday, more relaxation, and less sleep deprivation, they will actually get to class, learn better, and remember more.

Use with pages 67 and 68.

Name

LET ME CONVINCE YOU, CONTINUED

A convincing argument has several important components and takes careful planning. Choose a topic that excites and energizes you! It may be one shown here or any other appropriate topic.

Fill in the information below to get started.

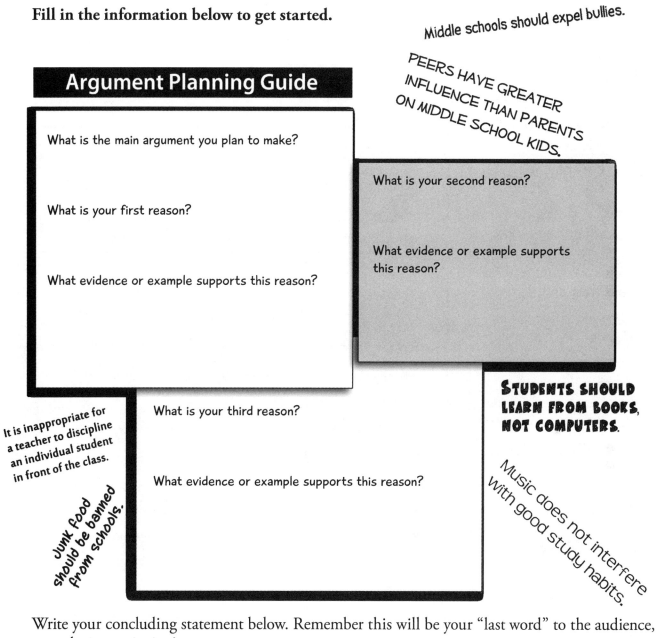

Middle schools should expel bullies.

PEERS HAVE GREATER INFLUENCE THAN PARENTS ON MIDDLE SCHOOL KIDS.

Argument Planning Guide

What is the main argument you plan to make?

What is your first reason?

What evidence or example supports this reason?

What is your second reason?

What evidence or example supports this reason?

What is your third reason?

What evidence or example supports this reason?

It is inappropriate for a teacher to discipline an individual student in front of the class.

Junk food should be banned from schools.

STUDENTS SHOULD LEARN FROM BOOKS, NOT COMPUTERS.

Music does not interfere with good study habits.

Write your concluding statement below. Remember this will be your "last word" to the audience, so make it convincing!

_____

_____

_____

Name

Use with pages 66 and 68.

Common Core Reinforcement Activities — 8th Grade Language

LET ME CONVINCE YOU, CONTINUED

Now use your plan from page 67 to write your argument. When you're finished, use the checklist while you revise and edit your work.

Argument Checklist

__My topic sentence clearly introduces my argument.

__I include reasons and evidence to support my claims.

__My reasons and evidence are logical, relevant, and accurate.

__I use transitional words, phrases, and clauses to make my argument flow smoothly.

__My word choice is appropriate for my audience.

__My conclusion summarizes my argument clearly and concisely.

__My spelling, grammar, punctuation, and capitalization are correct.

Name _____

Use with pages 66 and 67.

Copyright © 2014 World Book, Inc./ Incentive Publications, Chicago, IL

LET ME EXPLAIN

The primary goal of informative/explanatory writing is to convey information about an event, subject, idea, method, or issue.

Read this text to learn about skateboarding. Then use the next two pages to plan and write an informational/explanatory piece of your own.

Skateboarding is a popular sport and form of recreation in which an individual rides a small, narrow board mounted on four wheels, called a skateboard. The skateboarder balances on top of the deck (board) in the manner of riding a snowboard or a surfboard. Skateboarding is most popular among boys and young men. Professional skateboarders perform in competitions that are held on specially constructed ramps and obstacles. Some people use skateboards for transportation.

Any incline is my favorite place to be. If it's covered with snow, I'll grab my snowboard. Of course, I'm happy with a cozy couch, too.

A typical modern skateboard consists of six or seven layers of hard maple plywood. Urethane wheels and precision bearings permit smooth rides and gentle turns. For safety, skateboarders wear protective helmets, and sometimes knee pads, elbow pads, and wrist pads or gloves.

Skateboarding traces its origins back to scooters made of wooden crates in the 1920's. Skateboarding first gained popularity in the late 1950's with the growth of surfing. High-performance clay-wheeled skateboards appeared by the early 1960's, and urethane wheels were developed in 1973.

Work consulted:
Cave, Steve. "Skateboarding." *World Book Student.* World Book, 2013. Web. 11 Nov. 2013.
© World Book, Inc. Reprinted with permission. All rights reserved.

Name

Use with pages 70 and 71.

Text Types: Informative/Explanatory

Everyone has a special place they like to go to have fun, meet friends, or just relax. On the lines below, list a few of your favorite places. Then choose one and use this page as a guide to plan your explanation of the place you chose. Use the next page to write an essay that describes your place and explains why it is your favorite.

Explanatory Writing Planning Guide

What place are you going to describe?

List a few of your favorite places.

_____

_____

How will you introduce the place in a way that will get the audience's attention?

_____

_____

_____

How will you organize your information?

_____

_____

Put a star by one that you can use as the topic for a piece of explanatory writing.

What details, facts, and examples will you include?

What special vocabulary will you need to use?

The skateboard park has got to be one of my favorite places.

Will you need to include a graphic (like a map or a picture) to help your reader understand? If so, what will it look like and what information will it contain?

How will you conclude your piece in a way that helps your audience reflect on the information you've given?

_____

_____

Name

Use with pages 69 and 71.

LET ME EXPLAIN, CONTINUED

Now use your plan from page 70 to write your explanatory piece.
When you're finished, use the checklist while you revise and edit your work.

My Favorite Place _____

Explanatory Writing Checklist

___My topic is clearly introduced.

___My facts, details, and/ or examples are clear and appropriate for my audience.

___My organization is clear and logical.

___I use transitional words, phrases, and clauses to make my explanation flow smoothly.

___New or unusual vocabulary is explained.

___My conclusion summarizes my work clearly and concisely.

___My spelling, grammar, punctuation, and capitalization are correct.

Name

Use with pages 69 and 70.

LET ME TELL YOU A STORY

A narrative is a story, whether true or imagined. A good narrative has a setting, a plot, interesting characters, and descriptive details. Depending on the story's topic and mood, and the tone, it may also include such things as suspense, humor, adventure, or love.

Read the story below and try to picture the events in your mind as they unfold. Then use the next two pages to plan and write your own story.

It was finally here: sixth grade. No longer among the "little kids," I stepped off the bus and made my way through the front door of Abraham Lincoln Middle School. "This place is huge!" I thought, as I headed down the cavernous hall, glancing at all the room numbers in an attempt to find my first period class. My footsteps echoed on the blue linoleum floor and joined with the steps and voices of hundreds of others. Some were hanging out in small groups, confident and self-assured; those must be the eighth graders. Others seemed to be pretending to be confident, while some (including, sadly, me) were obviously lost and confused.

I looked everywhere for something familiar: a face, a place, a sign, anything. At that moment a hand tapped my shoulder.

"Lydia?" she asked.

"Hey!" I said. The red hair and slightly squeaky voice gave her away. It was Jasmine. Jasmine sat next to me for the last month of fifth grade and, while

we hadn't exactly been close friends, we had gotten along well. Now, at the sight of a familiar face, we acted as if we were reunited twins who had been separated at birth.

"It's so great to see you!" I said.

"You too!" she replied. "Can you believe the size of this place?"

And with that a friendship was formed. The two of us walked together to first period, and I thought to myself that middle school suddenly had become a little easier to navigate.

Name

Use with pages 73 and 74.

LET ME TELL YOU A STORY, CONTINUED

For your own narrative, tell a story about an encounter that changed your life.

Use the planning guide to get ready for your writing. Remember to think about the sensory details—sights, sounds, smells, tastes—when making your plan.

Narrative Planning Guide

Jot down some ideas about your life-changing encounter.

Be sure to answer these questions as you plan:

Where was it?

When did it happen?

What happened?

How did it end?

What did I learn?

How will your story begin?

Will this story be told from the first-person or third-person point of view? How will this point of view be introduced?

What details will you use to establish the setting?

How will you introduce the narrator and the characters? Will there be dialogue in your story?

How will your story be organized so that it's logical and makes sense to the reader?

What details will you include to help your reader picture the events?

How will you end the story?

Use with pages 72 and 74.

Name

Common Core Reinforcement Activities — 8th Grade Language

LET ME TELL YOU A STORY, CONTINUED

**Now use your plan from page 73 to write your story!
Use the blank oval for a cartoon, diagram, or other visual
to accompany the story. When you're finished, use the checklist
while you revise and edit your work.**

_____
_____
_____
_____
_____
_____
_____
_____
_____
_____
_____
_____
_____
_____
_____
_____
_____
_____
_____
_____
_____
_____
_____

Narrative Checklist

___ The beginning of my story grabs the audience's attention and makes them want to read more.

___ The events unfold naturally and logically.

___ The characters, including the narrator, are well developed and interesting.

___ I use a variety of words and sentence structures to engage my audience.

___ I include relevant descriptive details and sensory language.

___ Transitions make my sentences flow smoothly and keep the action moving.

___ My story has a conclusion that summarizes and/ or reflects on my life-changing encounter.

___ My spelling, grammar, punctuation, and capitalization are correct (including punctuating dialogue).

Name _____

Use with pages 72 and 73.

CONVERSATION CONVERSION

When your story, poem, article, or essay includes characters, the writing will be much more interesting if you include dialogue among the characters. Actual dialogue makes the writing come alive and helps the reader get to know the characters.

Writing dialogue properly (and punctuating it accurately) can be tricky! Below are three conversations. Convert them from their current form into written dialogue. Write your dialogue on the lines next to the comic strip.

WHAT A CHARACTER!

Characterization is the creating of characters for a story. A writer does this by describing the characters' actions, thoughts, and speech within the story.

How would you describe the characters below? Under each title, make a list of qualities, attributes, and words or phrases that you might associate with such a person. (Note the last one is blank. You fill in this title and illustration.)

An Ideal Friend

An Absolute Bore

A Curious Teenager

A Fun, Wacky Coach

A Mysterious Neighbor

Now choose one of these characters and use the outline on the following page (page 77) to plan a characterization.

Name

Use with page 77.

WHAT A CHARACTER!, CONTINUED

Use words and phrases collected on page 76. Create precise word pictures to show the character through his or her speech, thoughts, and behavior.

CHARACTERIZATION PLAN

I. A captivating title to command the reader's attention:

_____

II. A masterful opening statement to invite the reader to learn about my character:

_____

_____

_____

III. Follow-up sentences to introduce the major character traits:

_____

_____

_____

_____

IV. A strong body that will include these examples of actions and/or thoughts or speech to support statements made in the opening paragraph:

_____

_____

_____

_____

V. Ideas for a conclusion that will summarize the character and make the reader glad to have read the piece:

_____

_____

Name _____

Use with page 76.

ESCHEW OBFUSCATION

The report got a D- that I slaved over.

The title of this activity is a tongue-in-cheek expression that means, "Avoid making anything difficult to understand!" It's a good motto for writers! Careless writers cause all kinds of strange messages.

Repair the damage in these sentences by reworking each one to more clearly show its intended meaning.

1. While cleaning the attic this morning, a mouse scared me.

2. Paddling quietly along in the canoe, the moon shone brightly.

3. I read about the bank robbers who were caught in the morning paper.

4. While eating her cat food, Mom noticed that Fluffy had a burr in her paw.

5. As a child, my mother taught me many lessons.

6. There was a tiny cottage behind the junkyard that was very beautiful.

7. On the top shelf of my locker, I could not find my math book.

8. He sold ice cream sodas to the children with tiny umbrellas in them.

9. The eighth graders were punished after the fire alarm prank by the principal.

Name

THAT'S A GOOD QUESTION!

You may not realize it, but you conduct some type of research every day. You may be answering simple questions like, "What time does the game start?" or "How much will those concert tickets cost?" Or you may need to research more complex questions such as, "How do I find the right bicycle part to fix my bike, and how do I install it?"

Effective research writing involves consulting several reliable sources, paraphrasing or quoting appropriate information, and presenting your conclusions in a clear and concise manner with accurate citations. Here is a sample of research writing that answers the question,

"What was life like for early travelers on the Oregon Trail?"

The Oregon Trail was a 2,000-mile (3,200-km) route that ran from Independence, Missouri, to the Pacific Northwest. Travelers began using the Oregon Trail around 1843 in a quest to settle the West. The journey took about six months and was a true test of strength, endurance, and bravery. Groups of pioneers would buy wagons, oxen, and supplies in preparation for their journey. Then the difficulties would start. First, most travelers walked all 2,000 miles because the wagons were full of supplies and riding was bumpy and often painful. On the way, there were also numerous obstacles including harsh weather, diseases, dangerous river crossings, lack of drinkable water, and accidents. In fact, being run over by a wagon was the most frequent cause of injury and death! In total, approximately 20,000 travelers died over the length of the trail: that's an average of ten deaths every mile.

Works consulted:
"Chest of Hardships and Challenges." *ThinkQuest*. Oracle Education Foundation, n.d. Web. 1 Oct. 2013.
"Oregon/California Trails: Dangers." The National Oregon/California Trail Center, n.d. Web. 1 Oct. 2013.
"Oregon Trail." *World Book Online Reference Center*. World Book, 2013. Web. 1 Oct. 2013.

Here are some other history-related questions you may want to research:

• What role did women play in the American Revolution?

• What were the Salem Witch Trials and why were they important?

• What were some of the causes of the Great Depression?

• What was life like for Native Americans before European explorers arrived?

• Why was Benjamin Franklin an important figure in American history?

Use with pages 80 and 81.

Name

THAT'S A GOOD QUESTION!, CONTINUED

What is your question?_____

Fill in the table as you research. Use your classroom style guide for citations.

PARAPHRASE OR QUOTE OF DATA OR INFORMATION	SOURCES YOU WILL CONSULT AND CITE	ASSESSMENT OF SOURCE CREDIBILITY AND ACCURACY

What other questions were raised as you pursued this one?

_____

THAT'S A GOOD QUESTION! , CONTINUED

Now it's your turn to share what you learned. Use the lined area below to present your conclusions in a well-organized paragraph or two. Then use the oval for an illustration or other graphic to add interest to your writing. Cite (give credit to) your sources and consult the checklist while you revise and edit your work.

Research-Writing Checklist

___ My topic sentence refers to my original question.

___ I include evidence from multiple reliable sources.

___ I paraphrase or use quotations when needed AND cite the original source(s).

___ My ideas flow smoothly and are well organized.

___ My conclusion summarizes my ideas and makes my audience think.

___ My spelling, grammar, punctuation, and capitalization are correct.

Name

Common Core Reinforcement Activities — 8th Grade Language

ANOTHER VIEW

Changing the point of view from which a story is told can change the whole story! The narrator of this story is an anonymous witness to an incident. How would this situation appear to one of the characters present at the incident, or a character affected in some way by the incident?

Pay attention to the aspects of the story that might be unique to the particular viewpoint of the writer. Then follow the directions on the next page to show another point of view.

The Tortilla Incident

Tortillas flew at last Friday's pep rally in a silly prank that brought serious consequences to Ashville High. Students and staff are divided as to whether the joke was harmless or whether its perpetrators had malicious intent to humiliate the lower classmen.

According to several sources, the seniors on the varsity football team brought packages of soft tortillas to the pep rally and secretly distributed them to all students in the senior section of the gym.

The plan was to toss them into the freshman section as the freshmen took their turn at the school cheer. The plan worked. Each class took a turn at the cheer. When the freshmen began to cheer, the tortillas sailed. Many students screamed. Most students laughed. Faculty and staff members were not amused.

There were no reports of injuries. However, there was a flood of comments streaming into the principal. Many students felt this was an insult to the freshman class. Others saw it as a harmless prank. Dozens of parents felt the eventual punishment was too severe. Some felt the punishment should extend to the entire senior class.

Principal Arnold announced on Monday that all senior football team members would be suspended from school for one week and from the team for two weeks. In addition, she cancelled all pep rallies for the remainder of the year. This will no doubt have grave consequences for Ashville's chances at a championship football season.

Name _____   Use with page 83.

ANOTHER VIEW, CONTINUED

Re-tell the "Tortilla Incident" story from a different point of view. (This might be a freshman, a senior, a student of another level, a football player, the principal, or a parent.) Put yourself inside the mind of this witness (or nonwitness) as you tell the story.

Use this note to write a one-sentence comment to the principal as if it were sent from the narrator of your re-telling.

Use with page 82.

Name

QUOTES TO PONDER

Ponder the five quotes below; consider what each one means and whether you agree with it. All are statements made by famous Americans.

Choose three of the quotes and complete the chart below.

1.

"Three people can keep a secret if two of them are dead."

– Benjamin Franklin (1706-1790)

2.

"The earth is the mother of all people, and all people should have equal rights upon it."

– Chief Joseph (1840?-1904)

3.

"If you tell the truth, you don't have to remember anything."

– Mark Twain (1835-1910)

4.

"Enemies are so stimulating."

–Katharine Hepburn (1907-2003)

5.

"If there is no struggle, there is no progress."

– Frederick Douglass (1818?-1895)

Quote Number	Explain the quote in your own words.	Do you agree or disagree? Why?

Name

SPEAKING
AND
LISTENING

Grade 8

COLLABORATOR'S GUIDE

There are many times in school and beyond when you will need to collaborate with other people. Your group may need to work together to complete a project, make a decision, discuss a book, or accomplish some other goal.

No matter what the situation is, there are four actions that will help to make your collaboration the best it can be: **prepare, listen, respect,** and **respond.** Here are some guidelines to get you started. Have your group add their own ideas, too.

Prepare
- Be sure you understand the task.
- Know your role in the group.
- Research your topic.

Listen
- Pay attention to what your group members are saying.
- Have an open mind.
- Use encouraging body language.

Respect
- Look at people as they speak.
- Don't belittle anyone else's comments or answers.
- Don't interrupt or get distracted.

Respond
- Express your views clearly.
- If you don't understand something, ask clarifying questions.
- Give positive feedback when appropriate.

Name

COLLABORATOR'S GUIDE: PREPARE

Any group collaboration can be more successful if members are prepared!

Use this checklist to prepare for your discussion. Then fill out the *I'm Prepared!* form before you begin.

I'm Prepared!

Collaborator's Checklist

____ Be sure you understand the assignment and the goal(s) of the discussion.

____ Know how your discussion and its outcomes will be evaluated. (For example, ask yourself, "What are the expectations? What is the assignment?")

____ Do some research. Clarify any aspect of the topic you don't understand.

____ Prepare some questions you could ask other group members to keep the discussion going. Avoid questions that can be answered "yes" or "no."

____ Set one or two reasonable goals for yourself in the discussion (for example: How many times will you participate? Will you work on your eye contact, on not interrupting, or on drawing others into the discussion?).

I'm prepared!

Group Discussion Task:

What I have done to prepare:

Evidence I will contribute:

Questions I will ask:

My sources:

I've reviewed the rules for collaboration:

Name _____

COLLABORATOR'S GUIDE:
LISTEN, RESPECT, RESPOND

During a discussion, it is important that the group stays focused on the goals and every member contributes. One way to accomplish this is to have one group member serve as a recorder, making tally marks or notes on a chart like this one, as the discussion progresses.

Before the discussion, fill in this information:

Group members and their roles:

Discussion topic, question, issue, or task:

Goals and deadline:

During the discussion, keep track of members' participation on the chart.

NAME OF GROUP MEMBER	CONTRIBUTED NEW INFORMATION	ASKED A QUESTION	BROUGHT A NEW MEMBER INTO THE DISCUSSION	ACKNOWLEDGED NEW INFORMATION	BROUGHT THE DISCUSSION BACK ON TRACK
(example) Bob	/ / / /	/ /		/ /	/

After the discussion, answer these questions as a group:

1. What aspects of the discussion did our group do well?

2. What aspects do we need to work on next time?

3. Did we accomplish our task or goal?

This has been very helpful.

Name

COLLABORATOR'S GUIDE: REFLECT

After your discussion, it is always helpful to think about how you did.

Look over the chart from page 88 for your group. On your own, fill in the speech bubbles below.

Name

Common Core Reinforcement Activities — 8th Grade Language

LISTENER'S GUIDE

We are bombarded by sounds every day: people talking, car engines roaring, dogs barking, phones ringing, and many more. But what happens when you need to get *information* from something you hear (such as a video, a speech, or a demonstration)? What's the difference between just hearing something and *really listening?*

Listening is active. That means you have to do more than just hear the sounds; you have to use your brain to make sense of what you're hearing. You may also have to summarize ideas as you hear them or take notes to help you remember what you've heard.

Here is a guide to help you become a great listener:

1. Anticipate what you're going to hear and what information you want to prepare your brain to listen for. "What's the topic? Who is speaking? Who is the intended audience? What am I supposed to learn?"

2. Stay focused on the task and avoid distractions.

3. Listen for main points and details.

4. Look for patterns in the information— does the speaker repeat important points? Or use certain body language to emphasize a point?

5. Watch for any visual aids or demonstrations that enhance the information.

6. Repeat important facts inside your head after you hear them.

7. Take notes if possible.

I'm listening . . .

8. Write down any questions you have while they're fresh in your mind.

9. Be prepared to summarize what you've heard.

10. Be able to explain what you learned and how it helped you understand a new topic or clarify something you already knew.

Name

I LISTENED! I WATCHED! I LEARNED!

Use this form to respond to what you heard in any oral presentation.

Presentation Response Form

The main purpose of this presentation was...

The main idea was...

Details or examples that supported the main idea were...

Another key idea was...

Details or examples that supported this idea were...

How was the information presented?

What were the motives behind this presentation? (Explain your answer.)

What specific things from the presentation helped you clarify a topic or issue about which you already knew something? (Explain your answer.)

Were there nonspoken components that added to the message? These might include pictures, video, diagrams, or demonstrations. If so, what did they contribute to the presentation?

What did you learn from this presentation?

Name

Common Core Reinforcement Activities — 8th Grade Language

A HOOPING GOOD TIME: A LISTENING TASK

To the teacher: Use this essay and the accompanying graphic as a listening task. Read the essay or choose another reader to present it. Provide students with the illustration by projecting it or supplying it in print form to each student (but delete the other text from the page). Students can complete the Presentation Response Form on page 91 after listening to the passage.

Few toys have captured the attention of kids of all ages like the Hula-Hoop®. The first Hula-Hoop was introduced to the public in 1958, but the origins of a hoop-like toy go all the way back to 1000 BC, when Egyptian children made them out of dried grapevines. Hoop rolling was also a popular game in ancient Greece and Rome, and Native Americans used hoops for both entertainment and rituals.

Today, Hula-Hoops are used for games, dancing, exercise and more. There are weighted hoops, fire hoops, lighted hoops, and – if you're up for it – record-setting hoops. The Guinness Book of World Records lists 20 separate records for Hula-Hooping, including "the longest human chain to pass a Hula-Hoop" (249 participants), "most revolutions Hula-Hooping in one minute" (211), and "longest time to balance a Hula-Hoop on the head while swimming" (49 seconds). It would seem that this simple device continues to fascinate and entertain people all around the world.

Works Consulted:
Guinness World Records. "Hula Hoop." *GuinnessWorldRecords.com.* Guinness World Records, n.d. Web. 28 September 2013
Lamb, Robert. "How Hula Hoops Work." *HowStuffWorks.com.,* HowStuffWorks, 25 July 2011. Web. 28 September 2013.

Hula-Hoops for adults are 40 inches in diameter (102 cm). Children's Hula-Hoops are 28 inches in diameter (71 cm).

Cia Granger of Finland is a Hula-Hoop superstar! In 1999, she kept 83 Hula-Hoops going at the same time. Amazing!

Ken Kovach spun the most Hula-Hoop revolutions while somersaulting and jumping on a trampoline.

Ashrita Furman holds a record for the longest time to Hula-Hoop underwater— 2 minutes, 38 seconds.

Ashrita Furman ran a mile (1.6 km) in 13 minutes, 37 seconds with a milk bottle on his head while spinning a Hula-Hoop.

Name

I HEAR YOU

There are many people out there trying to convince you about a variety of topics: advertisers, politicians, enthusiasts for organizations, salespeople, parents, and even friends. This is done in speeches, ads, magazines or newspapers, arguments, videos, on the Internet, or in other media. Learning to listen critically to an argumentative presentation is a vital skill that will help you make decisions for yourself.

These questions will help you listen carefully and evaluate argumentative presentations for yourself. Take notes as you listen.

What was the speaker's topic?

What argument was the speaker making about this topic?

What claims did the speaker make to back up the argument?
(For each claim, ask yourself: "Was the reasoning logical? Was the claim relevant to the argument? Was there reliable evidence to back up the claim? Was there any irrelevant evidence? Was there enough evidence to convince you?")

Did the speaker leave you with unanswered questions?

People have become too dependent on technology.

College athletes should be paid.

All citizens should be required by law to vote.

All students should be required to speak a foreign language to graduate from high school.

Drunk drivers should be imprisoned on the first offense.

Dieting makes people fat.

You must have whiter teeth to be attractive.

Standardized tests should be abolished.

Name

REFLECTION ON AN ARGUEMNT

After listening to and evaluating an argument, it is important to reflect on what you heard, what you learned, and whether or not you were convinced.

Use this graphic organizer to reflect on a speech you have heard. Use any notes you took on the previous page.

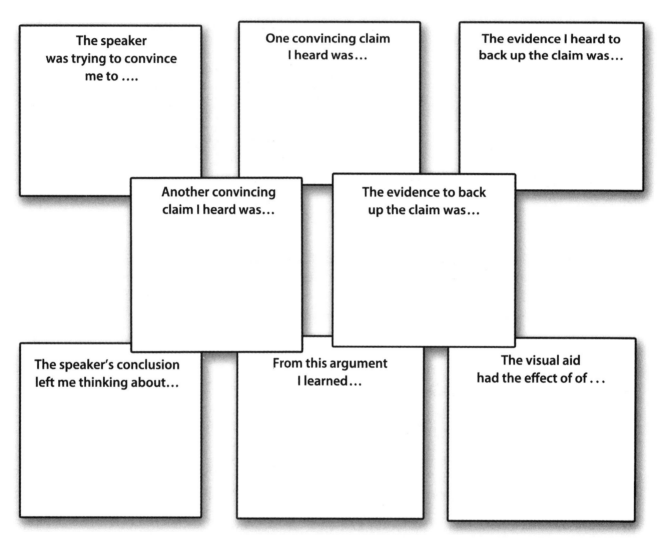

The speaker
was trying to convince
me to ....

One convincing claim
I heard was…

The evidence I heard to
back up the claim was…

Another convincing
claim I heard was…

The evidence to back
up the claim was…

The speaker's conclusion
left me thinking about…

From this argument
I learned…

The visual aid
had the effect of of . . .

Use the scale to rate each item below, with 1 being low and 5 being high.

Overall the speaker's reasoning was sound.   1   2   3   4   5

The speaker had enough evidence.   1   2   3   4   5

The speaker convinced me.   1   2   3   4   5

Name

SPEAKER'S GUIDE

Every great speech has two important components: **content,** or what you say, and **delivery,** or how you say it. Both of these components work together to make an impact on your audience.

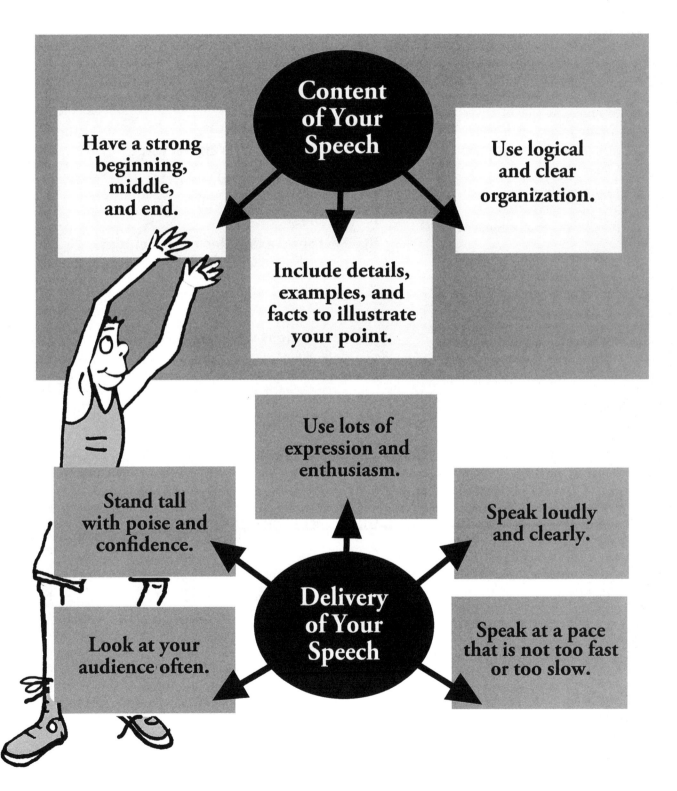

Content of Your Speech

Have a strong beginning, middle, and end.

Use logical and clear organization.

Include details, examples, and facts to illustrate your point.

Delivery of Your Speech

Use lots of expression and enthusiasm.

Stand tall with poise and confidence.

Speak loudly and clearly.

Look at your audience often.

Speak at a pace that is not too fast or too slow.

Name

Common Core Reinforcement Activities — 8th Grade Language

PLANNING A GREAT SPEECH

For this activity, you will be preparing and giving a three- to five-minute speech related to westward expansion in America (1800's). You will speak in the character of a person from that era.

Here's how it works:

1. First, INVENT a fictional character that is somehow related to westward expansion. For example,
   - a traveler on the Oregon Trail
   - a Native American
   - a witness at the Alamo
   - a mountain man or woman
   - a store owner in Independence, MO

2. Next, add some details to your invented character, including name, age, situation, and important personality traits.

3. Next, it's time to RESEARCH! Find facts, authoritative details, and relevant examples to your character's information. Make yourself "come alive!" Focus on what makes you different from every other person. Is it your personality? What are your hobbies and talents? What part do you play in the historical events? Be creative!

4. Now you're ready to **become** this character and **tell your story** to the class in the form of a first-person narrative speech. Be sure to include a strong beginning, middle, and end. Use the space here to begin planning. Take notes on a separate sheet (or use note cards). Create a visual aid.

5. Before you take the stage, PRACTICE! Use the Speaker's Guide on page 95 and the *How Was My Speech?* form on page 98 to guide you as you prepare.

I. **My character is**

II. **Details about the character:**

III. **Facts and examples I will include:**

IV. **Visual aids I will use:**

V. **How I will begin:**

VI. **Points I will make:**

VII. **How I will conclude:**

Name

REFLECTING ON MY SPEECH

Answer the following questions in complete sentences.

Speech topic or title_____Date: _____

- **What part** of this speech assignment was the easiest for you? (Think about creating the idea for a character, researching, taking notes, organizing, giving the speech, etc.) Explain your answer.

- **What part** of this assignment was the most difficult for you? Explain your answer.

- **What part** of your speech leaves you feeling the most proud? Why?

- **What two areas** do you need to improve when you make speeches in the future?

    1.

    2.

- **What is the most important thing** you learned from this speech assignment?

Name _____

HOW WAS THE SPEECH?

Use this form (including the scale at the bottom of the page) to evaluate each other's speeches. Be sure to include comments and suggestions.

Speaker:_____ Date: _____

Topic or Assignment:_____

Content (What was said?)

Introduction	1	2	3	4	5
Body	1	2	3	4	5
Appropriate facts and details	1	2	3	4	5
Realistic fictional character	1	2	3	4	5
Organization	1	2	3	4	5
Conclusion	1	2	3	4	5

Delivery (How was it said?)

Confidence and poise	1	2	3	4	5
Eye contact	1	2	3	4	5
Volume and clarity	1	2	3	4	5
Pace	1	2	3	4	5
Expression and enthusiasm	1	2	3	4	5

Comments and suggestions for the speaker:

Scale

5 points = Excellent! No improvements needed..

4 points = Very good. Only a little improvement needed.

3 points = Average. This is an area to work on.

2 points = Below average or hardly present at all. Needs more work.

1 point = Not present or unable to be heard. Needs lots of work!

Name

LANGUAGE

Grade 8

TREATS TO EAT

Rides are the main attractions at an amusement park, but doesn't everybody love all the fun food, too? So get ready to enjoy the goodies!

The title of this page contains an infinitive. The second sentence (above) has one, too. This sentence has two more: "If these kids are going to order cotton candy, they have to stand in line." Can you find all the infinitives?

> An **infinitive** is a verb form, usually preceded by the word **to.**
> It may be used as a **noun, adjective,** or **adverb.**
> An **infinitive phrase** combines an infinitive with its related words.

Circle the infinitives in the opening paragraph and in these sentences. UNDERLINE any infinitive phrases:

1. I love to munch popcorn.

2. To locate the cotton candy stand is my first priority.

3. It's not a great idea to ride the rollercoaster right after eating pizza.

4. Doesn't the ice cream seem to melt fast?

5. The popcorn smells like it's about to burn.

6. We want to eat treats all day long!

For each picture below, write a sentence that includes an infinitive phrase.

7. _____

_____

_____

8. _____

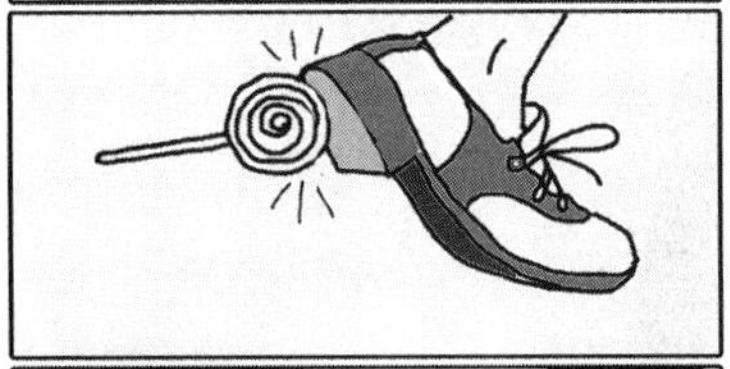

_____

_____

9. _____

_____

_____

10. _____

_____

_____

Name

JUGGLING GERUNDS

Exploring, riding, screaming, eating, watching, waiting, performing, juggling, singing— these are some of the many gerunds you might hear or do at the amusement park.

> A **gerund** is a verb form, ending in *ing*, that is used as a **noun.**
> Like a noun, a gerund can be used as a **subject (S),**
> **predicate nominative (PN),**
> **direct or indirect object (DO or IO),**
> or **object of a preposition (OP).**
> A **gerund phrase** is a gerund with all of its related words acting together as a noun.

Circle the gerund in each sentence. On the line provided, write the code (from the grey box) to tell how the gerund is used in the sentence.

_____ 1. Juggling is only one of the tricks the clown performed.

_____ 2. I like playing the carnival games.

_____ 3. At the point of turning, the roller coaster is fastest.

_____ 4. One of my favorite pastimes is watching people.

_____ 5. Unfortunately, waiting our turn took lots of time.

_____ 6. Once we got on *The Twister,* we loved riding.

_____ 7. What are the requirements for entering the water slide?

_____ 8. We gave screaming all out energy.

_____ 9. The most common motion on rides is spinning.

_____ 10. After leaving the ride, my stomach continued whirling.

Write a gerund phrase to complete each sentence below.

11. _____ is a difficult task.

12. Most kids love _____.

13. _____ seemed to excite the teenagers, too.

14. The problem _____ was one we had to solve quickly.

Name _____

TENSE TIMES

On *The Flume,* as on many other amusement park rides, times can get tense. This ride plunges through a narrow gorge, drops over a waterfall, and causes plenty of thrills and chills for its riders.

Active verbs will help you tell the story of any daring ride adventure. Conjugate each verb in all its *active* tenses.

RIDE

present   I _____

past   I _____

future   I _____

present perfect   I _____

past perfect   I _____

future perfect   I _____

SCREAM

present   We _____

past   We _____

future   We _____

present perfect   We _____

past perfect   We _____

future perfect   We _____

RUMBLE

present   It _____

past   It _____

future   It _____

present perfect   It _____

past perfect   It _____

future perfect   It _____

RUN

present   They _____

past   They _____

future   They _____

present perfect   They _____

past perfect   They _____

future perfect   They _____

Name _____

GET ACTIVE!

An amusement park is all about action! Lights flash, voices scream, people bustle, rides clatter. It's a perfect place for active verbs.

A verb is in **active voice** when the subject **performs** the action.
A verb is in **passive voice** when the action **is performed on** the subject.

Example: Passive: The ice cream was eaten by me.
             Active: I ate the ice cream.

Get the passive voice out of the amusement park (and out of these sentences)! Re-write each one with a verb in active voice.

1. Weren't you shocked by the speed of the drop on the *Alpine Plunge?*

2. The noise was almost drowned out by the squeals of passengers.

3. Was the lemonade spilled by you?

4. The *Spinning Dragon* has never been ridden by us.

5. Have all the tickets been confiscated by you?

6. The *Corkscrew* roller coaster was screeching to a stop.

7. Was the hot weather tolerated by your friends?

8. This place will be visited by us again!

9. We were awed by the colorful lights.

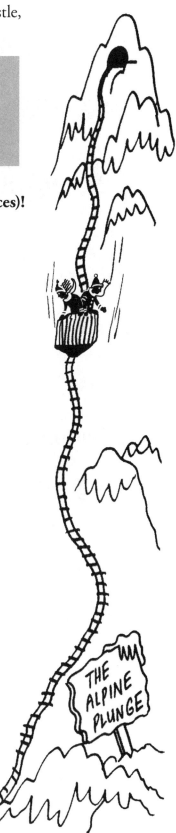

THE ALPINE PLUNGE

Name

Common Core Reinforcement Activities — 8th Grade Language

SETTING THE MOOD

The **mood** of a verb refers to the manner in which a thought is expressed or intended. Three commonly used moods are:

Indicative mood - verb expresses a statement
Example: *Creepy noises radiate from the creaky house.*

Imperative mood - verb expresses a request or command
Example: *Watch out!*

Interrogative mood - verb (along with a helping verb) asks a question, with the main verb coming after the subject
Example: *Are you brave enough to go inside?*

Passengers on a ride through the *Haunted Mansion* are greeted with a blood-curdling mood. Watch for the mood of the verbs as you read about this attraction.

Each sentence below uses its verb in the indicative mood. Re-write the sentence so that the verb is either imperative or interrogative.

1. The creaky car heads into dark shadows.

2. This ride is part thrill and part terror.

3. I feel a ghost rushing past my hair.

4. Spine-chilling screams fill the air.

5. I prefer to sit in the front seat.

6. I rode for the first time three years ago.

7. Since then, it's the first ride I take every time.

8. It's worth the wait in line.

9. Sometimes, I ride four or five times.

10. Even then, I still want more.

Name _____

Use with page 105.

SETTING THE MOOD, CONTINUED

Circle the entire verb in each sentence. Then decide the mood of the verb: indicative, imperative, or interrogative. Write the verb in the matching room on the floor plan of the haunted mansion.

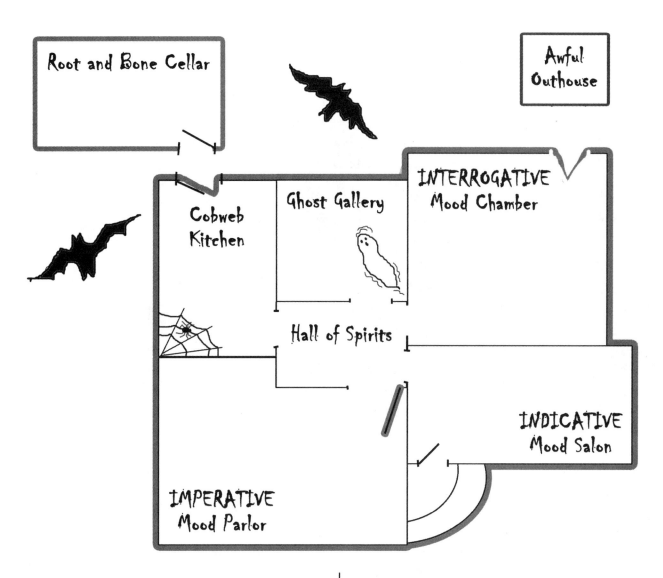

1. The trip through the *Haunted Mansion* has been nerve-racking.

2. Next time, I'll choose another ride.

3. Did you hear the moans?

4. Look at those shadows over there.

5. Is this becoming creepier?

6. I'll take your picture with that ghoul.

7. Will we be going up that staircase?

8. I am relieved that this is over.

9. Are you still shaking?

10. Go on the *Haunted Mansion* ride again!

Use with page 104.

Name

Common Core Reinforcement Activities — 8th Grade Language

TO RIDE OR NOT TO RIDE

Are you planning to try that new ride called *Nausea?* Maybe—or maybe not! You might use the subjunctive mood of a verb to talk about this decision.

The **subjunctive mood** of a verb is used to express a doubt, a wish, an opinion, a possibility, something that might happen, or something contrary to fact. It is often used in sentences with the words *urgent, important, require, essential, wish, suggest, ask, might, could,* or *would.*

Use the plural form of a verb for the subjunctive mood, even where the third-person singular would normally be used.

Examples: *It is urgent that each rider understands the risk.*
If I were you, I'd think twice before riding.

Look at each sentence on the ride. If it is correct, write OKAY in the oval. If the sentence is incorrect, change it to use the subjunctive mood correctly.

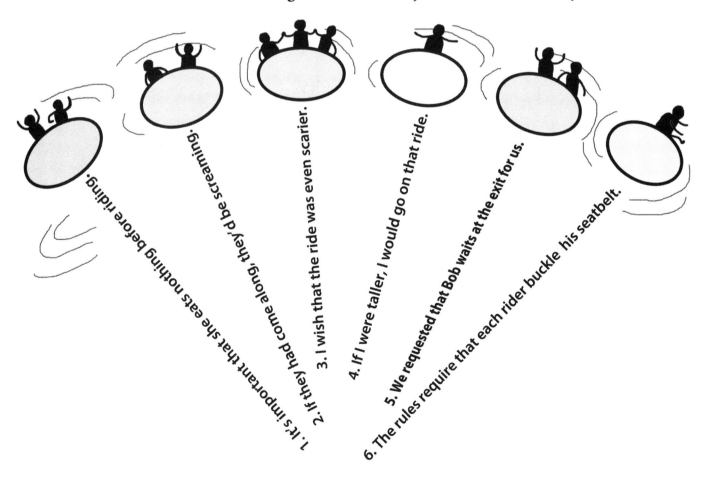

1. It's important that she eats nothing before riding.

2. If they had come along, they'd be screaming.

3. I wish that the ride was even scarier.

4. If I were taller, I would go on that ride.

5. We requested that Bob waits at the exit for us.

6. The rules require that each rider buckle his seatbelt.

Name

AVOIDING SHIFTS

If you want to toss a ring onto a bottle, it's important to keep a steady hand, avoid crazy throws, and be consistent. When you write a sentence or paragraph, it is important to keep verbs consistent. For example, if you start a sentence in the active voice, you should continue to use the active voice throughout the entire sentence. The same is true for verb tense and mood.

Look for improper shifts in voice, tense, or mood. If you fine them, re-write the sentences, keeping the verbs consistent.

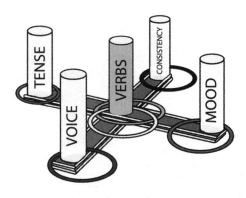

1. Jenna held the ring in her hand, then tosses it toward the target.

2. When she throws the ring, she watched it go.

3. A clanking noise was heard when the ring hit the bottle.

4. Aim more carefully, then she should toss the ring again.

5. The prizes looked great, and their display was seen by everyone.

6. Jenna's friends spent ten minutes watching her, but leave her alone after that.

7. Finally she held her prize high, and her award was worn with pride.

8. Jenna enjoyed the ring toss, but other activities were preferred by her friends.

Name _____

A PAUSE IN THE ACTION

Some friends are taking a break from their adventures in order to capture some pictures. The right punctuation can help sentences take a break.

Each of the following statements includes a pause or break. Decide whether a comma or a dash is more appropriate. Write your choice in the blank. In each blank speech balloon, write your own statement. In two of them, use a comma to indicate a pause. In the other two, include a dash.

The **comma** can be used to indicate a pause or break in a sentence. The **dash** can serve a similar purpose, acting like a "strong comma" when you want to add emphasis, signify an interruption, or show an abrupt change of thought.

1. Luke smiled for the picture _____ but Jill was making a face.

2. I wish you would stand still _____ oh never mind.

3. The photo looked awesome _____ focused, colorful, and fun.

4. After I took your picture _____ I shared it with everyone.

5. I'll gladly be in the next picture _____ as long as you make me look good!

6.

7.

8.

9.

MERRY-GO-ROUND AND ROUND

No amusement park or carnival is complete without a carousel (also known as a *merry-go-round*). Read about the background and history of this fascinating ride. Then brush up on one fascinating kind of punctuation—the ellipsis.

An **ellipsis** is a series of three dots that can be used to indicate that something has been taken out of a sentence. You can also use an ellipsis to shorten a direct quote (but not to change the quote!).

Example:
Original sentence: *On the merry-go-round,* which was beautiful, we sat on horses.
With an ellipsis: *On the merry-go-round…*we sat on horses.

Read this passage about merry-go-rounds. Choose three sentences and re-write them below, omitting some information and adding ellipses.

A merry-go-round is a popular children's ride at amusement parks, carnivals, and theme parks. The ride is also called a *carrousel* (also spelled *carousel*). A merry-go-round basically consists of brightly painted horses and other animals mounted on a circular platform. Benches that resemble chariots may also be mounted on the platform. Riders sit on the animals and benches. A motor causes the platform to revolve. Some animals are attached to poles that move up and down as the ride moves. On most merry-go-rounds, a mechanical organ plays music while the ride is in motion.

The merry-go-round is the oldest amusement ride still in use. The term *merry-go-round* first appeared as early as 1729 in a poem in an English newspaper. The first known American merry-go-round was operated in Salem, Mass., in 1799.

Work cited:
James, George W. "Merry-go-round." *World Book Online Reference Center.* World Book, 2013. Web. 6 Oct. 2013.
© World Book, Inc. Reprinted with permission. All rights reserved.

1.

2.

3.

Name

A JUNGLE CREWS (OR CRUISE)?

Take a boat trip through the jungle to show your spelling skills.

Choose a word to correctly complete each sentence.

WEATHER   WHETHER   ADVICE   EMINENT   IMMINENT   ADVISE   CAPITOL   CAPITAL   THOUGH

1. Our school _____ took us on a field trip to the amusement park.

2. The park is close to the _____ building of our state.

3. The _____ was perfect for a day at the park.

4. We started the day with a jungle _____.

5. The boat was not at all _____.

6. We rode along, getting a _____ look at the jungle life.

7. Suddenly, two crocodile _____ interrupted the trip.

8. I didn't realize we were in _____ danger!

9. Fortunately, I'm okay, _____ for the teeth marks on my arm.

10. I've got some good _____ about jungle-touring behavior.

CURSE   CRUISE   CREWS   PRINCIPLE   INCIDENCE   THROUGH   THOROUGH   PRINCIPAL   STATIONARY   STATIONERY   INCIDENTS   ACCEPT   EXCEPT

Name

LANDLUBBERS BEWARE!

The lines are long for *Captain Blackbeard's Adventure Ride,* but we're told the ride is worth the wait! Learn all about it, but watch out for danger in the form of confusing words.

Circle any misspelled words. Write them correctly on the lines below.

Ahoy, Mates! Don't miss Captin Blackbeard's Adventure Ride! Join Percy the Parrott as you try to outsmart the seasoned pirate, Blackbeard, and uncover a tresure hidden in the heart of the Carribbean. As you climb on board your ship, darkness will suround you. If your very quite, you can hear your sales filling with wind. Percy will help you on your quest for riches, as you use a compas and stars to navigait. Rember to keep a lookout for sharks or dangrous storms (and perhaps the occassional crocadile) as you make your way deep into the night. Bewear! Blackbeard is in persuit of the vary same tresure. You will need to be an expert captian to avoid his crew of outcasts and his notorious canon. Those he capchures are forsed to walk the plank. Those who find the berried treasure will have fond memries of there adventure.

_____ _____ _____ _____

_____ _____ _____ _____

_____ _____ _____ _____

_____ _____ _____ _____

_____ _____ _____ _____

Name

ACTION-PACKED ADVENTURES

A day at the amusement park is full of action. These photographs have caught some of it.

Write a short paragraph as a caption to accompany each picture. Use active verbs. (Circle all the verbs you use.) Keep the verb form and mood consistent throughout each paragraph.

1.

_____
_____
_____
_____
_____

2.

_____
_____
_____
_____
_____

3.

_____
_____
_____
_____
_____

Name

112

SURROUNDED BY CLUES

This vocabulary exercise is set in the context of an amusement park. Words are set in a context, too. A word in a sentence is surrounded by words and ideas that can give clues to its meaning.

Read each sentence. Find the bold word. Circle or highlight clues that can help you infer the meaning of the bold word. Write your guess for its meaning. Use a dictionary to check your guess for the actual definition.

1.
Your **ingenious** scheme worked to get us near the front of this line to *The Terminator.*

2.
Only **dauntless** passengers dare to try this dangerous ride.

3.
With great **trepidation**, and against my better judgment, I'm getting on this ride.

4.
My sister had a **dearth** of tickets left, so she has gone to buy more.

To The Terminator

Guess:

Definition:

Guess:

Definition:

Guess:

Definition:

Guess:

Definition:

5.
Some **patrons** skipped this ride because the tickets were too expensive.

Guess:

Definition:

6.
Stop pushing in line—you'll **instigate** a fight!

Guess:

Definition:

Name

RIDE THE RAGING RIVER!

Read the comments of a group of friends as they take a ride on the *Raging River Rampage.* Look closely at the context of each bold word.

Write your guess for the meaning of the word in bold type.

1.

I'm nervous about the **sinister** grins on the faces of my friends who have been on this ride before!

Guess: _____

2.

We were lucky that the guide was **adept** at steering our boat.

Guess: _____

3.

Scott's mouth was **agape** and his face was white when he saw the wave coming toward us.

Guess: _____

4.

The **arrogant** girl next to us thinks she knows everything.

Guess: _____

5.

The park officials do not **condone** standing up in the boats.

Guess: _____

6.

I didn't believe you, but now I **concede** that no one can keep dry on this ride.

Guess: _____

7.

Look at those giant muscles on the **herculean** ride operator.

Guess: _____

8.

"I **abhor** screaming tourists," said Buster, "even when I'm one of them."

Guess: _____

Name _____

THE BIG LOOP

The *Loop-the-Loop* roller coaster challenges riders with the thrill of an upside-down trip, again and again. The center of the loop is filled with root words. You'll use them to complete a word challenge!

Use your knowledge of root meanings and prefixes to create a word to match each definition below. Use the roots and prefixes inside the loop. (The spelling of some words or prefixes may need to change.)

_____ 1. against gravity

_____ 2. find a way around

_____ 3. structure beneath

_____ 4. break a connection

_____ 5. beyond the usual

_____ 6. throw away

_____ 7. measure around

_____ 8. send across

_____ 9. turn back

_____ 10. all knowing

_____ 11. carry away

_____ 12. line up again

_____ 13. see from afar

_____ 14. away from the rails

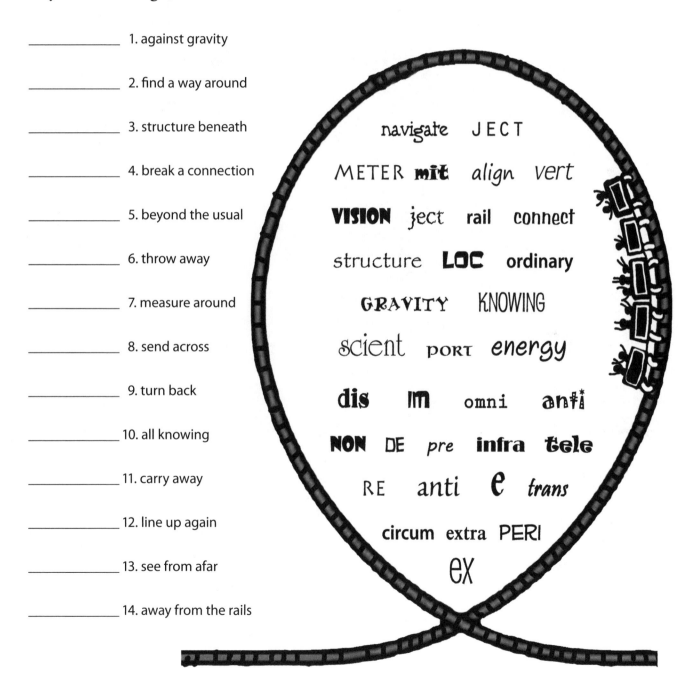

A MYSTERY TRAIN

What is the name of this wild train ride? Riders don't find out until the end of the ride. Get to the end of this ride by solving the word puzzle.

Create a word to match each clue by adding a suffix to a root. When you have all the answers, transfer the letter that matches each number to the space at the bottom of the page. If you have the answers right, these letters will spell the name of the ride!

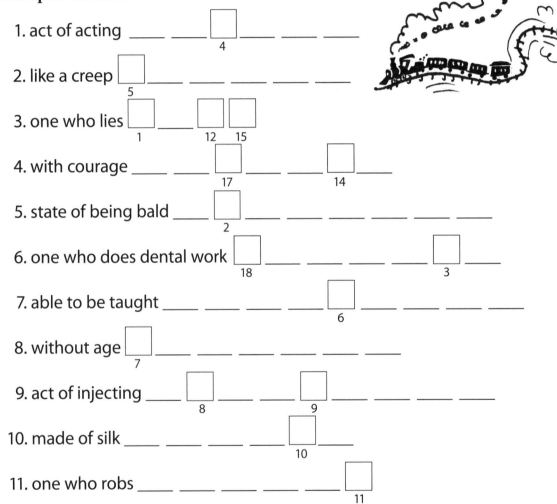

1. act of acting ____ ____ ☐ ____ ____ ____
                            4

2. like a creep ☐ ____ ____ ____ ____ ____
             5

3. one who lies ☐ ____ ☐ ☐
              1   12 15

4. with courage ____ ____ ☐ ____ ☐ ____ ____
                          17   14

5. state of being bald ____ ☐ ____ ____ ____ ____ ____
                           2

6. one who does dental work ☐ ____ ____ ____ ☐ ____
                            18   3

7. able to be taught ____ ____ ____ ____ ☐ ____
                                        6

8. without age ☐ ____ ____ ____ ____ ____
             7

9. act of injecting ____ ☐ ____ ____ ☐ ____ ____ ____
                       8   9

10. made of silk ____ ____ ____ ____ ☐ ____
                                    10

11. one who robs ____ ____ ____ ____ ☐
                                    11

12. to cause to have a motor ____ ☐ ____ ____ ____ ☐ ____ ____
                                16   13

____ ____ ____ ____ ____ ____ ____ ____ ____ ____ ____ ____ ____ ____ ____ ____ ____ ____
 1   2   3   4   5   6   7   8   9   10   11   12   13   14   15   16   17   18

Name _____

PLENTY OF CONFUSION

The Tower of Confusion thrills riders as it spins them into a dizzied frenzy! Here are some words that add to the spirit of confusion! It's easy for people to get them mixed up.

Use a dictionary to straighten out the confusion between the two bold words in each question. Circle the right answer.

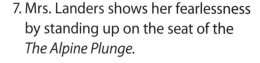

1. Molly predicts that Jake will get over his nausea from *The Tower of Confusion*.

   Is this a **prognosis** or a **diagnosis**?

2. Your fear seems to be spreading to everyone.

   Is it **contagious** or **infectious**?

3. Sam said, "I tell you! I do not want to go on *The Heartstopper*."

   Is his message **explicit** or **implicit**?

4. The famous Captain Hook is featured in the *Walk-the-Plank* ride.

   Is he **notorious** or **nefarious**?

5. Scott's enthusiasm about this ride is growing by the minute.

   Is his enthusiasm **waxing** or **waning**?

6. I'm just wild about rollercoasters. I've been on them all!

   Does Jayne have a **mania** or a **phobia**?

7. Mrs. Landers shows her fearlessness by standing up on the seat of the *The Alpine Plunge*.

   Is she **flaunting** her courage or is she **flouting** it?

8. The music from the rides is choppy and disconnected.

   Is it **staccato** or **legato**?

9. Kids have thrown stuff overboard from the rafts in the river.

   Is this floating material **jetsam** or **flotsam**?

10. Tom is full of energy as he climbs up *The Tower of Confusion*.

    Is he feeling **rigorous** or **vigorous**?

11. The roller coaster is climbing up to the top of the mountain.

    Is it heading for the mountain's **nadir** or **zenith**?

12. From watching you on these rides, I conclude you're not afraid of heights.

    Am I **inferring** or **implying** this?

Name

Common Core Reinforcement Activities — 8th Grade Language

WHAT WOULD YOU DO WITH IT?

Would you take a cygnet on a carousel? Or would you do something else with it? To decide what to do with something, you'll need to know what it means!

Use a dictionary to find the meanings for the bold words. Then circle the one choice that is appropriate for each word.

1. **cygnet**	take it on a carousel	put a leash on it	watch it swim	fry it
2. **fricassee**	sleep in it	bandage it	eat it for supper	curl it
3. **acronym**	write it down	weigh it	sit on it	cut it
4. **bijou**	put it on a sundae	water it	display it	broil it
5. **incisor**	put it in the bank	color it	swallow it	brush it
6. **felon**	slice it	wash it	arrest it	save it
7. **pique**	put it in an envelope	climb it	lasso it	get over it
8. **hellion**	give it a bath	burn it	paint it	discipline it
9. **serum**	have a party in it	read to it	put it in a test tube	broil it
10. **heirloom**	insure it	destroy it	dance with it	bury it
11. **annuity**	cage it	run from it	invest it	blow it up
12. **oxymoron**	bandage it	measure it	laugh at it	cure it
13. **bugaboo**	give it a haircut	fear it	fill it with helium	swat it
14. **gazette**	put it in a zoo	put jam on it	swat a fly with it	mow it
15. **foil**	fight with it	tickle it	melt it	memorize it

Name

DON'T TRY THIS AT HOME!

Each of these warnings is good advice.

Read each one to decide what it means. Use a dictionary to verify the meanings of words in bold type. Then tell why it would NOT be a good idea to do each of these things.

Is that an abutment
down there?

1. Don't bungee jump into an **abutment**.
   Why not?

2. Don't drink **brackish** water.
   Why not?

3. Don't try to sleep in **bedlam**.
   Why not?

4. Don't **jostle** a hippopotamus.
   Why not?

5. Don't go swimming in a **quagmire**.
   Why not?

6. Don't try to **hoodwink** a **pugilist**.
   Why not?

7. Don't be **vociferous** in a library.
   Why not?

8. Don't paddle a boat into a **maelstrom**.
   Why not?

9. Don't become a **sycophant** to a **hoodlum**.
   Why not?

10. Don't **procure** the services of a **pilferer**.
    Why not?

11. Don't **thwart** a lion's attempt to eat lunch.
    Why not?

12. Don't **jeer** at your older brother's haircut.
    Why not?

Name

Common Core Reinforcement Activities — 8th Grade Language

OVER THE EDGE

A day at the amusement park has pushed Molly over the edge. Her story is told with the help of figurative language. ***Figurative language*** uses words or phrases in a way that departs from their literal meanings. Writers use this tool to create special effects—adding other layers of meaning to the text.

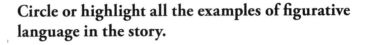

Circle or highlight all the examples of figurative language in the story.

I'm still soggy!

Poor Molly has gone off her rocker. We've decided that she's lost all of her marbles and has bats in her belfry. This day at the amusement park started off as a red-letter day. We got off on the right foot with a great ride on *The Wild Mouse.* Everyone in the group was having more fun on the rides than a barrel of monkeys. But, by ten o'clock, the tide had turned for Molly. She had blown her top at least eight times. First, on *The Screaming Eagle,* she lost her cool when she had to sit in the last car. Then, she got as sick as a dog on *The Scrambler* and gave us all a tongue lashing for taking her on the ride. Next, she was madder than a wet hen when her hair and clothes got soaked on *The Raging River Rampage.* And when Scott put his foot in his mouth and said her hair looked gruesome, she lost her head completely and started screaming bloody murder.

I think the last straw was the snow cone down her back. She ran around like a chicken with its head cut off, raking us over the coals and yelling about how we were driving her up the wall. We really tried hard to get her to cool her jets, but she just kept telling us to get off her back. Being with her was as much fun as going to the dentist.

Finally, she chilled out a little and wandered around in a fog for a while. We tried to keep the lid on things so she wouldn't flip out completely. Just when it seemed like the heat was off, some out-to-lunch little kid cut right ahead of her in line to *Into the Deep,* the submarine ride that was her favorite. Molly went totally bananas. In her frenzy, she fell right into the mermaid pond. Lucky for her, Scott pulled her out in the nick of time—just as an oncoming submarine was about to cream her!

Choose four of your favorite examples. Write or tell someone what each one means.

Name

CASTLES IN THE AIR

A trip through *Sir Glance-a-lot's Castle* follows a trail of idioms. These are figurative expressions whose meanings cannot be detected from the actual words.

Find the meaning of each idiom in the castle. Join with one or two classmates to share your understanding of the meanings. Choose one of the idioms to illustrate. In the corner space, draw something to show its literal meaning.

5. I got the answer straight from the horse's mouth.

11. You crack me up!

6. THANKS! YOU LEFT ME HOLDING THE BAG!

12. I THINK SAM GOT UP ON THE WRONG SIDE OF THE BED.

1. She's always building castles in the air.

7. We're caught between the devil and the deep blue sea.

2. Josh is usually behind the 8-ball.

8. You're just beating a dead horse.

13. We'll be here till the cows come home.

3. We're up a creek without a paddle.

9. He's in the doghouse now.

4. I've been burning the candle at both ends.

10. Lucy's barking up the wrong tree.

Name _____

FIND THE IMPOSTER

In this Hall of Mirrors, the words in each mirror have something in common—all the words except one, that is! Can you find the words that don't belong?

In each of these mirrors, four of the five words have something in common. Decide on the common classification. Write it near the mirror. Then put an X through the word that does not belong.

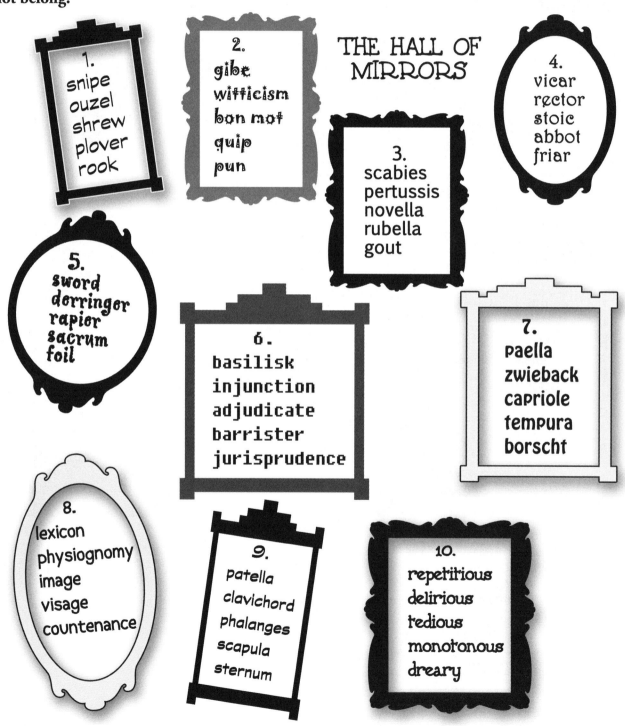

THE HALL OF MIRRORS

1.
snipe
ouzel
shrew
plover
rook

2.
gibe
witticism
bon mot
quip
pun

3.
scabies
pertussis
novella
rubella
gout

4.
vicar
rector
stoic
abbot
friar

5.
sword
derringer
rapier
sacrum
foil

6.
basilisk
injunction
adjudicate
barrister
jurisprudence

7.
paella
zwieback
capriole
tempura
borscht

8.
lexicon
physiognomy
image
visage
countenance

9.
patella
clavichord
phalanges
scapula
sternum

10.
repetitious
delirious
tedious
monotonous
dreary

Name

DOUBLE THE FUN

The Stomach Wrencher ride travels up and down with steep dives, then jerks from side to side with hairpin curves. If your stomach can handle it, you can have twice the fun! But after you ride, you might want to try a calmer attraction. Find and circle the one word in each group that is not related to the other words. Be ready to explain the relationship of the words in the group.

Synonyms are words that have the same or nearly the same meaning. Circle a pair of synonyms in each sentence and you'll have the answer to the question that follows.

1. You become ebullient on *The Stomach Wrencher*. Are you ecstatic or nauseous?

2. The lady next to you on that ride is looking languid. Is she robust or weak?

3. Tadd's got a grueling job. Is it torturous or leisurely?

4. You enjoy a canapé. Have you eaten an appetizer or watched a good comedy?

5. A person full of avarice has trouble with which of these: indigestion or greed?

6. When you gore a shrimp, do you stab it or sell it?

7. Your mom says that you masticate loudly. Are you too noisy when you snore or chew?

8. You laugh at a fatuous friend. Is he clever or foolish?

9. When you gnash your teeth, do you brush or grind them?

10. If your studying is futile, is it productive or useless?

11. Your hat is garish. Is it tasteful or flashy?

12. Your neighbor is churlish. Is she funny or grumpy?

13. A pain in your side is acute. Is it ticklish or severe?

14. You grow up to be renowned. Are you famous or handsome?

15. You are glutted after lunch. Are you tired or stuffed?

16. Some people fidget during the opera. Do they wiggle or snore?

He said
he felt bilious on
The Stomach Wrencher.
Was he feeling
queasy or
talkative?

Name

Common Core Reinforcement Activities — 8th Grade Language

CONTEMPLATE CONNOTATIONS

Sam felt uneasy as he waited to get on *The Twister.*

What if one of these sentences was used to replace the one above?

> **Sam felt dread as he waited to get on** *The Twister.*
> **Sam felt distressed as he waited to get on** *The Twister.*
> **Sam felt terrified as he waited to get on** *The Twister.*

Wouldn't you get more of a sense that Sam was really scared?

That's because the connotations of these words suggest more fear than is suggested by the word uneasy. Even when words have similar meanings, the connotations can give entirely different impressions.

For each example, tell how the connotation of the bold word in the second sentence changes the meaning.

1. Ramon was **eager** for *The Twister* ride to be over.

   Ramon was **desperate** for *The Twister* ride to be over.

   _____

   _____

2. She reached out to me with **slender** fingers.

   She reached out to me with **scrawny** fingers.

   _____

   _____

3. Tom showed **pride** after winning the prize.

   Tom showed **conceit** after winning the prize.

   _____

   _____

4. Anne gave her little sister a **disapproving** look.

   Anne gave her little sister a **hateful** look.

   _____

   _____

5. The teenagers **discussed** their neighbors.

   The teenagers **gossiped** about their neighbors.

   _____

   _____

6. As we waited in line, the sun **burned** our skin.

   As we waited in line, the sun **scorched** our skin.

   _____

   _____

Name _____

BEYOND DENOTATIONS

The words in each group below have similar denotations (definitions) but somewhat different connotations (associations).

Write the denotation and the connotation for each word. Then join with some classmates to discuss the differences in connotations for the words in each group.

Word	Denotation	Connotation
fireworks		
explosion		
illuminations		
nauseous		
sick		
afflicted		
happy		
delighted		
content		
predicament		
catastrophe		
difficulty		

Name

Common Core Reinforcement Activities — 8th Grade Language

HARD-WORKING WORDS

There are some words that show up again and again in assignments, tests, reading tasks, and research projects. To be a successful student, you need to be able to DO the action or process that the words name. But first, you must understand what the words mean!

Match each word with the phrase that explains what it means. Then get together with one or more classmates and DO several of the actions to show that you can put these words to work.

A. think through, break into pieces

B. figure out, read between the lines

C. judge, find the value of

D. tell about

E. tell the main points or ideas

F. list the ways things are alike

G. list the ways things are different

H. make an educated guess about what could happen

I. arrange according to class or category

J. show

_____ classify

_____ summarize

_____ compare

_____ describe

_____ infer

_____ EVALUATE

_____ demonstrate

_____ contrast

_____ PREDICT

_____ ANALYZE

Name

ASSESSMENT AND ANSWER KEYS

ENGLISH LANGUAGE ARTS ASSESSMENT

PART ONE: READING

The Fox and the Wood-cutter

A Fox running before the hounds, came across a Wood-cutter felling an oak, and besought (begged) him to show him a safe hiding-place. The Wood-cutter advised him to take shelter in his own hut. The Fox crept in, and hid himself in a corner. The huntsman came up, with his hounds, in a few minutes, and inquired of the Wood-cutter if he had seen the Fox. *He declared that he had not seen him, and yet pointed all the time he was speaking, to the hut where the Fox lay hid.* The huntsman took no notice of the signs, but, believing his word, hastened forward in the chase. As soon as they were well away, the Fox departed without taking any notice of the Wood-cutter: whereon he called to him, and reproached him, saying, "You ungrateful fellow, you owe your life to me, and yet you leave me without a word of thanks." The Fox replied, "Indeed, I should have thanked you most fervently, if your deeds had been as good as your words, and if your hands had not been traitors to your speech."

Work cited:
Aesop. "The Fox and the Wood-cutter." Trans. George Fyler Townsend. *Three Hundred and Fifty Aesop's Fables: Literally Translated from the Greek.* Chicago: Belford, Clarke & Co., 1885. 125-26. Print.

1. How does the author initially present the Wood-cutter in relationship to the Fox?

2. What does the italicized sentence reveal about the Wood-cutter's true intentions?

3. What is the effect of the final dialogue on the plot of the story?

Write the meaning of each word within the story context:

4. **hastened** (sentence five)

6. **fervently** (final sentence)

5. **reproached** (sentence six)

7. **traitors** (final sentence)

Name

Fire and Ice

-Robert Frost

Some say the world will end in fire,

Some say in ice.

From what I've tasted of desire

I hold with those who favor fire.

But if it had to perish twice,

I think I know enough of hate

To say that for destruction ice

Is also great

And would suffice.

Work cited:
Frost, Robert. "Fire and Ice." *American Poetry 1922: A Miscellany.*
New York: Harcourt, Brace and Co., 1922. *Google Books.* Web. 7
Nov. 2013.

What is the meaning of these words in the poem?

8. **perish** -

9. **suffice** -

10. What human attitude or behavior is represented by fire?

11. What human attitude or behavior is represented by ice?

12. What viewpoint(s) does the poet show?

13. How does the rhyme add to the poem's overall effect?

14. Write a summary of the poem.

Name

Rap music is a form of popular music that is generally spoken or chanted at a fast pace rather than sung. Rap is performed over musical accompaniment that emphasizes rhythm rather than melody. Often, this accompaniment consists of short segments of previously recorded music combined in new patterns. Rap music often features clever rhymes, word play, and lyrics that are made up on the spot.

The term *rap* is frequently used to mean *hip-hop,* but the second term includes more than just music. Hip-hop is part of a modern urban lifestyle. The term is used to describe a culture with both visual and audio elements, such as clothing, rapping, disc jockeying, break dancing, language, and graffiti. Hip-hop music is often more melodic than pure rap.

The biggest inspiration for rap came from disc jockeys in Jamaica, who would *toast* (talk) over recorded music they played in clubs. The style, known as *dub,* produced popular records that featured disc jockeys talking over instrumental backgrounds and electronic effects. The disc jockey used records on two turntables, switching rapidly between them to mix and match beats. This style was introduced into New York City clubs and became a part of the music more regularly heard in the clubs.

American rap music developed in the mid-1970's in New York City. It soon spread to other urban areas, primarily among African American teenagers. Rap grew rapidly in popularity in dance clubs in the late 1970's as disco music began to lose its following among dancers. The style soon spread throughout the United States and much of the world.

As with rock music before it, the lyrics of rap and hip-hop music have often been controversial. Some critics see a recurring theme of violence toward women in the songs. The videos of rap and hip-hop artists also have been criticized for violence and strong sexual content.

The first rap hit was "Rapper's Delight" (1979) by the Sugar Hill Gang. "The Breaks" (1980) by Kurtis Blow helped spread rap among a wider audience. Much of early rap expressed a party spirit. But such performers as Public Enemy looked harder at social issues and were often angry and aggressive. A style known as *gangster rap* or *gangsta rap* emphasized gunplay and other outlaw aspects of urban life.

In some variations of rap and hip-hop, artists have returned to the reggae music of Jamaica for inspiration. Mainstream rock artists have tried to incorporate elements of rap into their music by inviting rappers to perform on their records. Popular rap performers have included the Beastie Boys, Dr. Dre, Eminem, 50 Cent, Ice-T, Jay-Z, Lil Wayne, OutKast, Queen Latifah, Run-D.M.C., and Snoop Dogg.

Work cited:
McKeen, William. "Rap music." *World Book Student.* World Book, 2013. Web. 2 Nov. 2013.
© World Book, Inc. Reprinted with permission. All rights reserved.

15. What is the purpose of this text?

16. Underline or highlight phrases that identify key ideas that support the purpose.

17. How does the structure help accomplish this purpose?

Name

TOWN CENTER ROCK CONCERT

10 PM – MIDNIGHT
PROGRAM

BE A LITTLE BOULDER, HONEY
CURT MCCAVE

PLEASE DON'T TAKE ME FOR GRANITE, BABY
THE STANDING STONES

I'M YOURS TILL THE VOLCANO ERUPTS
LULU AND THE LAVA-ETTES

INTERMISSION

YOUR LOVE IS LIKE A SABER-TOOTH TIGER
TERI DACTYL AND THE HOT ROCKS

I DINO IF YOU LOVE ME ANYMORE
TOMMY SHALE

YOU'RE AS CUDDLY AS A WOOLLY MAMMOTH
SMASHING MARBLES

YOUR HEART'S MADE OF PETRIFIED WOOD
MICK JAGGED AND THE ROLLING BOULDERS

I'VE CRIED PEBBLES OVER YOU
ROCKY AND THE MARBLES

GRAVEL PIT ROCK
THE PALEO-LYTHS

18. What is the double meaning of "Rock" in the title?

19. What is the purpose of this text?

20. What is the tone? How can you tell?

21. Circle at least five examples of puns. Choose two to explain.

22. Identify two examples of figurative language (other than puns).

23. How are all the events on the program connected?

Name _____

Common Core Reinforcement Activities — 8th Grade Language

Dear Editor:

It's about time your newspaper had something in it besides country music news! Thousands of people in this city are interested in economic, social, and political issues; sports; theater; dance; and other kinds of music. But we are constantly bombarded with the life stories, gossip, awards, accomplishments, finances, and troubles of personalities and companies in the country music industry. I've heard enough of the financial woes, relationship blunders, and bad judgment of the "glamorous" crooners. You're about to lose my subscription. By the way, I have another beef: the delivery of my paper is inconsistent and too costly.

I fully understand that the country music business is a major and important part of this city's economy and the cornerstone of our tourist industry. However, you have not billed this paper as a music industry gazette—not a tabloid or fan magazine. Your website describes the paper as "covering diverse topics and appealing to diverse viewpoints." *The Daily Times* has a county-wide readership. You need to appeal to an audience beyond those who want to hear about broken hearts and miserable lives!

Yours truly,
Lester McGrath

24. What is the author's claim?

25. What relevant evidence does he use to support his claim?

26. Is any irrelevant evidence introduced into the argument? If so, what?

27. Are you convinced of his position? Tell why or why not.

Name

PART TWO: WRITING

1. Everybody loves a good mystery. Put your narrative-writing skills to work to write a short one. Get your inspiration from one of the ideas below or create one of your own. Start with a breath-taking beginning that sets the stage and engages the reader right away. Give some ideas that might be clues. Build the suspense! Wrap up with an interesting and satisfying resolution.

_____

_____

_____

_____

_____

_____

_____

_____

_____

_____

- a note or valuable item that suddenly appears or disappears
- something is wrong, missing, found, weird, or hidden
- strange noises or unusual smells
- a locked room or a secret room
- whispers, shrieks, or bizarre noises from the walls
- shifting shadows
- a creepy cellar, attic, or garage
- lights flashing, moving closer
- a cell phone (or computer) with a mind of its own

FOLLOW THE CLUES, INC.

Name

2. Write a clear explanation of how to break a habit. Choose a habit, real or imagined. Start with an opening statement about the habit and a bit about why it's problematic. Then give practical steps to follow to stop the habit. End with a summarizing conclusion.

_____

_____

_____

_____

_____

_____

_____

_____

_____

_____

3. "Fashion is for people who need someone else to tell them who they are."

Take a position agreeing or disagreeing with this quote by a 10th grader. Write a convincing argument in favor of your opinion. Add supporting details. Include a dynamic opening and closing.

_____

_____

_____

_____

_____

_____

_____

Name _____

PART THREE: LANGUAGE A—Conventions

Circle the verbal in each sentence (a gerund, gerund phrase, participle, participial phrase, infinitive, or infinitive phrase). Explain how it is used in the sentence.

1. Skiing off a cliff is not a good idea. _____

2. Jamal and Devon were tired of following marked trails. _____

3. These bored teenagers decided on a foolish course. _____

4. The skier suspended in thin air is Jared. _____

5. Now, the skiers are terrified to land on solid ground. _____

Identify the verb voice as active (A) or passive (P).

_____ 6. We were shocked by the height of the drop!

_____ 7. Devon landed a few feet from a huge tree.

_____ 8. Both skiers plunged deeply into the powder.

_____ 9. Fortunately, their falls were softened by the soft snow.

_____ 10. "This trick will not be tried by us again," mumbled Devon.

Make necessary changes to correct shifts in verb mood, tense, or voice.

11. Ski Patrol members lifted Jared onto a stretcher, then will load him onto the snowmobile.

12. The rules require that each skier skis at his or her own risk.

13. The ambulance sped away and heads straight to the hospital.

14. Nurses met the ambulance and the patients were accompanied by them into the emergency room.

15. Take good care of them, and then you could talk to them about their reckless skiing.

Name _____

Circle the numbers of the sentences below in which commas, dashes, or ellipses are used correctly.

16. Hey, watch out for that tree—oh, it's too late!

17. When I saw the drop, I just tried to stay in control.

18. I'd take another trail . . . if only I had the chance.

19. Jared sailed off the edge . . . and awoke in the hospital.

20. My skis flew off—and my face hit the snow.

Find and fix the spelling errors in the headlines.

21. Skiers Survive Trecherus Desent

22. Young Athalates Found Consious in Ski Accadent

23. Docters Perform Emergensy Surgery

24. Snowfall Park Reports Eigth Rescu of the Season

25. Ski Hill Closses Dangerus Runs

26. Injurred Skiers Skied Outside Boundries

27. Skiers Ignoring Rules Will Forfit Season Passes

28. Skiers' Condishun Suprizingly Good, Doctors Say

Name

PART FOUR: LANGUAGE B—Vocabulary

Add prefixes and/or suffixes to form a word from each root. Write the meaning for each word you create.

1. act

_____

2. dynam

_____

3. mort

_____

4. pend

_____

5. cred

_____

6. port

_____

7. posit

_____

Use context clues to guess at the meaning of the bold word in each statement.

8. I was gliding along smoothly until a novice skier **thwarted** my progress.

9. Lulu, are you avoiding this hill because you're **skittish** around snowboarders?

10. You're wise to be careful around reckless, **inept** boarders.

11. Let's take a break from the **rigors** of our sport. I'm exhausted!

12. There's no break for me—not after the **inordinate** price I paid for my ticket!

Name

Describe the relationship between the two bold words in each sentence.

13. A cup of hot chocolate **relieves** my stress and **alleviates** my ankle pain.

14. This snow park is **infamous** for perilous trails and **notorious** for accidents.

15. I have an **excruciating** pain in my elbow and a **dull** ache in my ankle.

16. Should I **revive** that **vibrant** aerial ski-trick performance?

Circle the word that best finishes the analogy.

17. **Flurries : blizzard :: interested : ____**

   ignored   obsessed   snow   hobby

18. **Churlish : ____ :: fatuous : sensible**

   curly   pleasant   surly   silly

19. **Avarice: greed :: ____ : renowned**

   disowned   owned   feared   notable

20. **____ : chew :: gazette : read**

   incisor   newspaper   brush   molar

21. **Scalpel : ____ :: hoe : gardening**

   doctor   tool   surgery   incision

Circle the word with the connotation that best fits the sentence.

22. I'm _____ at the snowboarder who never even looked or slowed down, but ploughed into me—leaving me with a broken ankle.

   *annoyed   aggravated
   incensed   miffed*

23. I hate being immobile! I _____ to be back on my feet!

   *want   yearn
   aim   wish*

24. You just wait! I'll be back to my _____ snowboard tricks soon!

   *skilled   wonderful

   spectacular   lovely*

Name

ASSESSMENT ANSWER KEY

Part One: Reading

Answers will vary. Give credit for answers that adequately and accurately answer the questions and follow the instructions.

1. open-hearted, willing to help and protect the Fox
2. Secretly, through hand signals, the Wood-cutter betrayed the fox, telling the huntsman where the Fox was hiding.
3. The Wood-cutter ignored his own bad behavior, but the Fox pointed out the duplicity.
4. hurried
5. scolded
6. adamantly or energetically
7. betrayers
8. die
9. be enough, work
10. desire
11. hate
12. He is of two minds; he thinks perhaps desire is the most destructive human failing, but can see that hate, too, is destructive.
13. Rhyme makes the sounds interesting, helps the message flow. It also helps to distinguish between the two elements.
14. Two elements, fire and ice, could be responsible for the world's end. Both the fire of human desire and the ice of human hate are destructive. Either could win out.
15. to give some background and history about rap music
16. *Rap music is a form of popular music that is generally spoken or chanted at a fast pace rather than sung; the term* **rap** *is frequently used to mean* **hip-hop,** *but the second term includes more than just music; the biggest*

inspiration for rap came from disc jockeys in Jamaica, who would **toast** *(talk) over recorded music they played in clubs; American rap music developed in the mid-1970's in New York City. It soon spread to other urban areas, primarily among African American teenagers; the lyrics of rap and hip-hop music have often been controversial. Much of early rap expressed a party spirit. But such performers as Public Enemy looked harder at social issues and were often angry and aggressive; artists have returned to the reggae music of Jamaica for inspiration; mainstream rock artists have tried to incorporate elements of rap into their music*

17. Each of the short paragraphs adds information about a different element or topic: the definition, its connection to hip-hop, its history, its growth in America, the controversy surrounding it, the spirit of rap, and the spread into mainstream music. All the short pieces flow together to give a good, general overview.
18. rock music and rock as in the Stone Age and Earth's surface
19. to amuse, to play on words—taking a popular modern idea and setting it in another era
20. lighthearted, fun; the clever names of songs and groups and the word play/puns
21. There are many puns. Student choices will vary. Check for accuracy.
22. simile, metaphor (*Your Love Is Like a Saber-Tooth*

Tiger, You're as Cuddly as a Woolly Mammoth; I've Cried Pebbles Over You, Your Heart's Made of Petrified Wood)
23. All have song titles and group names connected to the Stone Age.
24. that the newspaper gives too much space and exposure to the country music personalities and business
25. Most of the "evidence" is personal assessment.
26. If, statistically, the claims are true, the evidence is mostly relevant. The beef about poor delivery and cost of the paper does not advance this argument.
27. Answers will vary. Look for evidence to support student's choice

Part Two: Writing

1 through 3: Student writing will differ. Check all passages to see that they are clear and flow smoothly and that they follow the directions adequately.

Part Three: Language A— Conventions

1. Gerund phrase: *Skiing off a cliff*; subject
2. Gerund phrase: *following marked trails*; object of preposition
3. Participle: *bored*; adjective
4. Participial phrase: *suspended in thin air*; adjective
5. Participle: *terrified*; predicate nominative OR infinitive phrase: *to land on solid ground*; direct object
6. P
7. A
8. A
9. P
10. P
11. Change *will load* to *loaded.*

12. Change *skis* to *ski.*
13. Change *heads* to *headed.*
14. Change *and the patients were accompanied by them* to *and accompanied the patients.*
15. Delete *you could.*
16.-20. Circle 16, 17, 19
21. Treacherous, Descent
22. Athletes, Conscious, Accident
23. Doctors, Emergency
24. Eighth, Rescue
25. Closes, Dangerous
26. Injured, Boundaries
27. Forfeit
28. Condition, Surprisingly

Part Four: Language B— Vocabulary

1.-7. Answers will vary. Some possibilities:
1. actor, active
2. dynamic, dynamite
3. mortal, mortician, immortality
4. suspend, depend, expend, pendulum
5. credible, credulous, incredible, credentials
6. portable, import, export
7. position
8.-12. Answers will vary. Some possibilities:
8. interrupted, stopped
9. nervous
10. unskilled
11. demands
12. high
13. synonyms
14. synonyms
15. antonyms
16. same root
17. obsessed
18. pleasant
19. notable
20. incisor
21. surgery
22. incensed
23. yearn
24. spectacular

ACTIVITIES ANSWER KEY

Note: There are many cases in which answers may vary. Accept an answer if the student can give a reasonable justification or details to support it.

Reading: Literature (pages 22–44)

pages 22-23

Possible answers:

1. *It was to be the paramount night of Joe's career; tonight he would be serving all 50 state governors; solely because of Joe's reputation; his famous linguine*
2. famous linguine, the many Italian items on the menu, the tiramisu, *insalata caprese*, basil aroma, marinara sauce, and the restaurant name
3. With the opening words *It was to be;* with the news that Mario had just fallen in love that day and was not paying attention well
4. A. an appetizer, a spreadable paste made from vegetables or meat
   B. fruit of the sea, fish
   C. most important
   D. huge

page 24

1. that if you are angry with someone and you do not tell them, the anger grows and becomes damaging
2. The anger, unchecked or unabated, becomes a poison that spreads harm.
3. The writer disguised his anger and appeared to be welcoming to the foe, so the foe came to be a friend—to take advantage of

the gift of kindness (the apple) that he thought was offered.

4. death
5. A. anger
   B. trickery
   C. enemy
   D. hidden

page 25

1. discovery of cheating
2. overhearing conversation (all of second and fourth paragraphs); *Serena cleverly positioned herself to make sure that Anne could see her paper.*
3. Jenny is an observer who has taken no action so far except to listen and watch.
4. It leaves the reader to hypothesize different endings and to wonder or discuss what he or she might do in such a situation.

pages 26-27

Setting: people's bathrooms; the setting drives the plot because this is where the mystery develops and where it is solved

Main Character: the dog, Lucy; adjectives will vary; the dog and its bathing is the central issue/conflict in the plot; this is where the mystery, investigation, and resolution meet.

Theme: baffling mystery; there were several cases—all the same, but no obvious suspect. There were no break-ins and no obvious motive.

Plot: A detective tries to

solve a strange mystery where a serial bather visits bathtubs all over town while people are on vacation. The detective discovers that a dog walker leaves his own old dog to soak in tubs while he gives exercise to the pets left at home by their owners.

page 28

adolescence; *adolescence, skin that lumps and bumps, bodies that burst out in awkward ways, friends betray you, trade you in for someone more important, self-esteem, teenagers don't get much of that (respect and admiration), someone (children) can look forward to being and a reminder to adults of who they were*

page 29

1. the names of the baseball players are unusual words such as Who, Why, Tomorrow, That; and when they converse, Abbot thinks he's asking questions using the normal meanings of those words but Costello uses the words to refer to the players.
2. Abbot wants to make sure Costello knows about baseball, since Lou is considering becoming a baseball player. He is persistent in trying to get the questions answered.
3. argumentative, irritated
4. Abbott doesn't

understand that Costello does not understand the players' names.

5. Answers will vary; it would probably not be nearly as funny as the back-and-forth of spoken dialogue.
6. Answers will vary.

pages 30-31

1. Pyramus: *talked in secret, met in the shadows, made a daring plan, he could no longer live without the freedom to see her, distraught with guilt, devotion for her*
2. Thisbe: *talked in secret, met in the shadows, made a daring plan, eager to hear his plan, she dreamed aloud, went to the chapel early, she could not let him die alone*
3. Student writing will vary. Check for accurate representation of the story conversation and for accurate writing of dialogue.

page 32

1. tantrum—tandem
2. extinguished—distinguished
3. unparalyzed—unparalleled
4. statue—stature
5. tudor—tutor
6. sciences—sinuses
7. evaporate—evacuate
8. contraptions—contractions
9. Putrefied—Petrified
10. historically—hysterically
11. Presbyterians—pedestrians

12. mockeries—monarchies
13. irritate—irrigate
14. Individual malapropism sentences will vary.

page 33

1. garbage
2. shy
3. danger
4. superb
5. cheap
6. Copy
7. ally
8. Retain
9. initial
10. monotonous

page 34

1. S, poor
2. D, teasing
3. R, spendthrift
4. D or C, rock
5. R, enraged
6. F, bucket
7. R, fetid
8. R, veteran
9. C, courtroom
10. W, injection

page 35

1. parched - dried
   yearn - long for
   succulent - juicy
   revitalizing - bringing back life
2. It's about water; many words and phrases describe the strength and urgency of being thirsty (lacking water) and the wonderful relief of water; the final line is the chemical expression for water.

pages 36-37

Students will find many similarities and differences.

Both poems share a theme, an urgency to be loved, and

a message that it is good to have love. The poem has lines, is shorter, uses metaphors, is written in a more formal style, does not tell about a specific relationship, and is written in first-person viewpoint. The prose is more casual, gives a personal story, and is written in second-person viewpoint.

Answers to the final question will vary. Look for clear explanations of the choice.

pages 38-39

1.-2. and 4. Answers will vary. Look for serious answers with reasons.

3. Humor is introduced with description of the garish dress of the knights and the way they talk to the king. In addition, the writer questions the honor and validity of the actual actions (brave duels) of the knights—painting them as somewhat frivolous.

page 40

Answers here will vary. Look for a complete summary that gets at the idea that slow and steady can overcome the impetuous and erratic. Look for connections between this story and current literature.

page 41

Jade: believes she was treated unfairly; not wanting to get her parents involved

Teacher: closed to the discussion of Jade's grade; sticking to strict procedure

Parents: upset, wanting to take action

page 42

As students will choose varying stories, the answers will vary. Check to see that the table has been filled in completely and that questions are answered completely.

Reading: Informational Text (pages 44–64)

page 44

Answers will vary.

Safe: (not all that much evidence); bungee cord stops a fall. "Assurance" that the elastic cord will save you from disaster. Many people have jumped successfully. More people are injured in car accidents.

Unsafe: reports of injuries to eyes and limbs, shock of the abrupt stop, many other injuries and deaths, jumper's error, lack of safety precautions, factors beyond the jumper's control.

page 45

1. to protect and preserve the world's oceans, waves, and beaches
2. drop in on
3. yes
4. The water hits a steep incline in the ocean floor topography with a greater force, pushing it upward so high that the top of the breaking wave curls forward with great force.
5. Diagrams will vary. Check them for understanding of the written text.

page 46

Facts: newest state, number of islands, length

of the state, only state completely surrounded by water, beaches and miles of warm surf, moderate temperatures, long hours of sunshine, beautiful sunsets, brilliantly colored flowers that bloom year round, tourists spot for people from all over the world, key products, recreation and tourism are main sources of income for many, first settlers brought Polynesian tradition, new arrivals have come, culture has additional facets and flavors

Opinions: most beautiful state, favorite playground of mainland Americans, dances and customs are the main source of beauty and richness, a fascinating place to live, a delightful place to vacation

Student reasons will vary. Look for sound explanations.

page 47

1. A town worked together to build a record-setting ice cream treat.
2. reference to the *loving care,* the residents of the town, and detailed description of the ice cream concoction
3. anyone in the area who could come to see the banana split
4. to attract visitors to the event
5. Choices will vary. Look for sound choices and explanations.

pages 48-49

Look for thorough completion of the organizer on page 49. Check to see that

students have identified evidence and details in each of the unshaded boxes.

page 50

1. moral perfection
2. He thinks he knows what is right and what is wrong.
3. It was more difficult than he thought. Habits and inattention crept in. While he was guarding against one fault, another caught him off guard.
4. He decides that he has to break bad habits and establish good ones before he can reach his goal of consistent good conduct.

Summaries will vary. Check to see that they make sense and state the main idea of the text.

page 51

Check to see that the diagram is completed to show the progression from butte to mesa to plateau, with explanations in the arrows as to how they are related.

pages 52-53

Answers will vary. Some possibilities are:

1. Opinions vary.
2. The long list, with so many items beginning with NO, gives an overwhelming feel of negativity, repression, and control. OR, the list form makes it easy to see the rules and get the message across.
3. Answers will vary. The text plus the notes plus the illustration show differences of opinions.

4. Answers will vary. This shows the reason why a dress code might be needed (sagging pants). It also could show that students don't want to pay attention to the dress code, or don't care.
5. a. suggested
   b. disregarded
   c. limiting
   d. guarantee
   e. unfair treatment of some groups
   f. wealthy

page 54

1. a. enemy
   b. past history
   c. hardship
   d. promise, guarantee
2. Answers will vary. Look for reasonable explanation for tone. (Tone could be serious, reassuring, challenging, or encouraging.)
3. Answers will vary. Look for reasonable explanation for answer. (The words support a message of strength, determination, sacrifice, and almost threat.)

page 55

Answers will vary. Look for student evidence and explanation of their answers.

1. passionate, awed
2. Words show awe and inspiration: *vastness, sublimity, grandeur, awesomeness, unique, expresses within that distance more than any one human mind yet has been able to comprehend or interpret, all alike have failed* (to portray or describe it), *but not so with the Grand Canyon*

3. that they all are words to describe that grandness of the canyon
4. within the understanding of man

pages 56-57

1. Principal Wimple—strongly displeased Ed Whelp, Dorothy Braidy—thought it was fun and harmless, or interesting Lisa Grummel—thought it was harmful some students (Ivan) found it scary
2. This gave information about the consequences for involved students.
3. Answers will vary. (made the story come alive; added humor)
4. Reports were that this was what started the food-fight, but they cannot be verified
5. things flying through the air
6. Consequences were being planned for punishing those responsible.

pages 58-59

1. dedicate—give attention and honor to consecrate—declare something special or holy or dedicate for a purpose hallow—sacred resolve—decide with determination, commit to perish—die
2. the history and commitment to freedom and democracy
3. The honor in the battlefield cannot be given by the onlookers or visitors; it is consecrated by the lives and sacrifice and blood of those who fought there.
4. Answers will vary. Look for strong explanations. Possible: to honor the people who fought and died and to promise that freedom will go on in their names
5. Answers will vary. Look for strong explanations.

pages 60-61

Look for completion of the graphic organizer that shows the student can examine, analyze, and evaluate an argument. Look for clear claim (that sagging does not belong in schools and perhaps should be banned in general), and identification of supporting evidence. Look for identification of relevant, sufficient or insufficient evidence, and explanation of why the student was or was not convinced. Look for two reasonable ideas the could support the opposite claim.

pages 62-63

Summaries will vary.
#1 Summary: There are ordinary explanations for most UFO sightings. No reliable evidence exists to confirm any extraterrestrial connection with the sights.
#2 Summary: Many UFO sightings are reported each year, including accounts from reliable sources such as military personnel and airline pilots.
#1 Facts: Many reports have come in. Weather conditions can create optical illusions. Investigators can explain all but a small percentage of UFO reports.
#2 Facts: Kenneth Arnold reported seeing a group of bright objects. A letter was sent to NASA with a sighting in 1962. Several websites are dedicated to UFO reports.
#1 Opinion: Sightings may be due to unknown phenomenon.
#2 Opinion: "It is the opinion of both (my companion) and myself that the object behaved so much unlike conventional aircraft . . ." Final question: answers will vary. Look for sound evidence in the answer.

page 64

Answers will vary. Check student responses to see that the explanation includes reference to the written text and the visual presentation—telling what was learned from integrating both kinds of information.

Writing (pages 66-84)

pages 66-68

Plans and writing will vary. On page 67, check to see that student has completed all sections of the Argument Planning Guide, identified reasons and evidence for each reason, and written a strong concluding statement. On page 68, check argumentative writing for indications of meeting the standards W.8.1a-e and for indication that student reviewed and applied the checklist to the writing.

pages 69-71

Plans and writing will vary. On page 70, check to see that student has adequately answered all questions in the Explanatory Writing Planning Guide and written a strong concluding statement. On page 71, check explanatory writing for indications of meeting the standards W.8.2a-f and for indication that student reviewed and applied the checklist to the writing.

page 72-74

Plans and writing will vary. On page 73, check to see that student has completed all parts of the Narrative Planning Guide adequately and written a strong concluding statement. On page 74, check explanatory writing for indications of meeting the standards W.8.3a-e and for indication that student reviewed and applied the checklist to the writing.

page 75

Check student dialogues to see that the main idea of the conversation has been translated into dialogue, and that the dialogue is punctuated and capitalized correctly.

pages 76-77

Characterizations will vary. Examine student products to see that they have brainstormed fresh, interesting words and phrases on page 76, and used them to complete the plan on page 77. The assignment does not ask for a completed characterization essay. It asks for a strong plan.

page 78

Student corrections of the sentences will vary. Possibilities:
1. A mouse scared me while I was cleaning the attic this morning.
2. As I paddled quietly along in the canoe, the moon shone brightly.
3. In the morning paper, I read about the bank robbers who were caught.
4. While Fluffy was eating her cat food, Mom noticed a burr in Fluffy's paw.
5. When I was a child, my mother taught me many lessons.
6. Behind the junkyard was a very beautiful, tiny cottage.
7. I could not find my math book on the top shelf of my locker.
8. He sold ice cream sodas with tiny umbrellas on top to the children.
9. After the fire alarm prank, the principal punished the eighth graders.

pages 79-81

Questions, research, and writing will vary. Check student writing for clear, interesting answers to the question, use of reliable information, and correct citations.

pages 82-83

Student stories will vary. Examine student work for indication of an understanding of point of view and a clearly presented point of view that differs from the story on page 82.

page 84

Responses will vary. Check to see that they

include indication of aspects of the text that fulfill the assignment and that students have provided evidence for their agreement or disagreement.

Speaking and Listening (pages 86-98)

pages 86-89

Check to see that students have adequately completed the Prepare, Listen, Respect, Respond, and Reflect parts of the Collaborator's Guide.

pages 90-92

Check student's Presentation Response Form (page 91) completed in response to the listening task on page 92. Look for complete, thoughtful answers that indicate careful listening.

pages 93-94

As students use these forms for critical listening to assigned presentations, review their responses for careful listening and adequate answers.

page 95-97

Review students' preparation notes and reflections for their own speeches. Look for a substantive planning outline on page 96 and thoughtful answers to self-reflection questions on page 97. Apply standards SL.8.4-6 in listening to their speeches.

page 98

Review student evaluations of each other's speeches to see that comments and suggestions support the numerical ratings.

Language (pages 100-126)

page 100

Infinitive in title: *to eat;* infinitive in opening paragraph: *to order, to enjoy;* infinitives in second paragraph: *to order, to stand*

1. to munch (to munch popcorn)
2. To locate (To locate the cotton candy stand)
3. to ride (to ride the rollercoaster right after eating pizza)
4. to melt (to melt fast)
5. to burn
6. to eat (to eat treats all day long)
7.-10. Answers will vary. Check to see that each sentence includes an infinitive phrase.

page 101

1. Juggling; S
2. playing; PN
3. turning; OP
4. watching; PN
5. waiting; S
6. riding; DO
7. entering; OP
8. screaming; IO
9. spinning; PN
10. whirling; DO
11.-14. Answers will vary. Check to see that each sentence includes a gerund phrase.

page 102

I ride; I rode; I will ride; I have ridden; I had ridden; I will have ridden

We scream; We screamed; We will scream; We have screamed; We had screamed; We will have screamed

It rumbles; It rumbled; It will rumble; It has rumbled; It had rumbled; It will have rumbled

They run; They ran; They will run; They have run; They had run; They will have run

page 103

Answers will vary. Possibilities:

1. Didn't the speed of the drop on the *Alpine Plunge* shock you?
2. The squeals of passengers almost drowned out the noise.
3. Did you spill the lemonade?
4. We have never ridden the *Spinning Dragon.*
5. Have you confiscated all the tickets?
6. The *Corkscrew* roller coaster screeched to a stop.
7. Did your friends tolerate the hot weather?
8. We'll visit this place again!
9. The colorful lights filled us with awe.

page 104

Answers will vary. Possibilities:

1. Will the creaky car head into dark shadows?
2. Expect thrills and terrors from this ride.
3. Get out of my hair, ghost!
4. Listen to the spine-chilling screams filling the air.
5. Sit in the front seat.
6. Has it been three years since I first took this ride?
7. Is this the first ride you take every time?
8. Get in line; it's worth the wait!
9. Have I ridden this four times—or five?
10. Will I still want more?

page 105

1. has been; indicative (Mood Salon)
2. choose; indicative (Mood Salon)
3. Did hear; interrogative (Mood Chamber)
4. Look; imperative (Mood Parlor)
5. Is becoming; interrogative (Mood Chamber)
6. will take; indicative (Mood Salon)
7. will be going; interrogative (Mood Chamber)
8. am relieved; indicative (Mood Salon)
9. Are shaking; interrogative (Mood Chamber)
10. Go; imperative (Mood Parlor)

page 106

1. Change *eats* to *eat.*
2. Change *they'd be* to *they would have been.*
3. Change *was* to *were.*
4. OKAY
5. Change *waits* to *wait.*
6. OKAY

page 107

Answers will vary. Possibilities:

1. Change *held* to *holds* OR *tosses* to *tossed.*
2. Change *throws* to *threw* OR *watched* to *watches.*
3. no change
4. Delete *she should.*
5. Change *their display was seen by everyone* to *everyone saw their display.*
6. Change *leave* to *left.*
7. Change *her award was worn with pride* to *she wore her award with pride.*
8. Change *other activities were preferred by her friends* to *her friends preferred other activities.*

page 108

1. comma
2. dash
3. dash
4. comma
5. dash
6.-9. Answers will vary. Check student examples for appropriate uses of the comma and dash.

page 109

Answers will vary. Check student examples for appropriate uses of the ellipsis.

page 110

1. principal
2. capitol
3. weather
4. cruise
5. stationary
6. thorough
7. incidents
8. imminent
9. except
10. advice

page 111

Circle misspellings of these; rewrite correctly: Captain, Parrot, treasure, Caribbean, surround, you're, sails, compass, navigate, Remember, dangerous, occasional, crocodile, Beware, pursuit, very, treasure, captain, cannon, captures, forced, buried, memories, their

page 112

1.-3. Captions will vary. Examine student responses for appropriate use of active verbs, consistent verb form, and consistent verb mood. Check to see that all verbs are circled.

page 113

Guesses will vary. Here are the definitions:
1. clever

2. fearless
3. fear and trembling
4. lack
5. customers
6. start or cause

page 114

Guesses will vary. Some possibilities are:
1. mean, evil
2. good, skilled
3. wide open
4. snooty, conceited
5. approve of
6. agree
7. extremely strong
8. dislike, hate

page 115

1. antigravity
2. circumnavigate
3. infrastructure
4. disconnect
5. extraordinary
6. eject
7. perimeter
8. transmit
9. revert
10. omniscient
11. export
12. realign
13. television
14. detail

page 116

1. action
2. creepy
3. liar
4. bravely
5. baldness
6. dentist
7. teachable
8. ageless
9. injection
10. silken
11. robber
12. motorize

Name of railroad is:
Last Chance Railroad

page 117

1. prognosis
2. contagious
3. explicit
4. notorious
5. waxing
6. mania
7. flaunting

8. staccato
9. jetsam
10. vigorous
11. zenith
12. inferring

page 118

1. watch it swim
2. eat it for supper
3. write it down
4. display it
5. brush it
6. arrest it
7. get over it
8. discipline it
9. put it in a test tube
10. insure it
11. invest it
12. laugh at it
13. fear it
14. swat a fly with it
15. fight with it

page 119

Explanations will vary. Check student responses for understanding of the bold word meanings. Definitions are:
1. abutment - a large, strong structure that supports something
2. brackish - salty
3. bedlam - chaos
4. jostle - push or bump against
5. quagmire - wet, soft ground (such as quicksand)
6. hoodwink - trick; pugilist - boxer
7. vociferous - loud
8. maelstrom - powerful whirlpool
9. sycophant - flatterer; hoodlum - crook
10. procure - hire, obtain; pilferer - thief
11. thwart - discourage, prevent
12. jeer - mock or treat rudely

page 120

Circle: off her rocker, lost all of her marbles,

has bats in her belfry, a red-letter day, got off on the right foot, more fun on the rides than a barrel of monkeys, the tide had turned, blown her top, lost her cool, as sick as a dog, gave us all a tongue lashing, madder than a wet hen, put his foot in his mouth, lost her head, screaming bloody murder, the last straw, ran around like a chicken with its head cut off, raking us over the coals, driving her up the wall, cool her jets, get off her back, as much fun as going to the dentist, chilled out, tried to keep the lid on things, flip out, the heat was off, went totally bananas, in the nick of time, about to cream her.

Task at the bottom: Check student explanations for understanding of the figures of speech.

page 121

Listen to student discussions and view their drawings. Look and listen for indications that they understand the meanings of the idioms and the difference between the literal and figurative meanings.
1. plans things that have little possibility of happening
2. is in trouble, in a tight spot
3. in a difficult situation with no help
4. been working too hard
5. straight from the source of authority
6. left me with the

responsibility because someone backed out
7. have two unappealing choices
8. trying to accomplish or persist in a lost cause
9. in a lot of trouble
10. looking for help in the wrong place
11. make me laugh
12. is grumpy
13. for a long time

page 122

1. birds; shrew
2. clever, funny verbal comments; gibe
3. diseases; novella
4. religious leaders; stoic
5. sword-like weapons; sacrum
6. legal terms; basilisk
7. foods; capriole
8. words that name or describe appearance; lexicon
9. body parts; clavichord
10. synonyms meaning boring; delirious

page 123

1. ebullient; ecstatic
2. languid; weak
3. grueling; torturous
4. canapé; eaten an appetizer
5. avarice; greed
6. gore; stab
7. masticate; chew
8. fatuous; foolish
9. gnash; grind
10. futile; useless
11. garish; flashy
12. churlish; grumpy
13. acute; severe
14. renowned; famous
15. glutted; stuffed
16. fidget; wiggle
Answer to question in art: bilious; queasy

page 124

Answers will vary. Check for student understanding of the shades of meaning and the differences between the two words used in each example.

page 125

Connotations will vary. Check for student understanding of the shades of meaning and the differences between the two word used in each example.
Denotations:
fireworks - brightly exploding chemicals
explosion - sudden loud noise releasing energy
illuminations - lighting up
nauseous - sick in the stomach
sick - unwell
afflicted - feeling distress
happy - feeling joy
delighted - highly pleased
content - satisfied
predicament - a difficult or unpleasant situation with no way out
catastrophe - a disaster
difficulty - a hard situation

page 126

Order of answers will be: I, E, F, D, B, C, J, G, H, A
A. analyze
B. infer
C. evaluate
D. describe
E. summarize
F. compare
G. contrast
H. predict
I. classify
J. demonstrate
Watch student/group actions as they show what the words mean.